COACHING CORPORATE

CORPORATE

MVPs

COACHING
CORPORATE
MVPs

CHALLENGING AND DEVELOPING
HIGH-POTENTIAL EMPLOYEES

MARGARET BUTTERISS

RIGHT
MANAGEMENT
A Manpower Company

JB JOSSEY-BASS™

Library and Archives Canada Cataloguing in Publication Data

Butteriss, Margaret
   Coaching corporate MVPs : challenging and developing high-potential employees / Margaret Butteriss.

Includes index.
ISBN 978-0-470-15312-3

   1. Employees—Coaching of. 2. Mentoring in business. 3. Employee retention. I. Title.

HF5549.5.C53B88 2008   658.3'124   C2008-900605-4

Production Credits
Cover design: Ian Koo
Interior text design: Natalia Burobina
Printer: Tri-Graphic Printing Ltd.

This book is printed with biodegradable vegetable-based inks. Text pages are printed on 60 lb TG Eco 100, 100% post-consumer waste.

John Wiley & Sons Canada, Ltd.
6045 Freemont Blvd.
Mississauga, Ontario
L5R 4J3

Printed in Canada

1 2 3 4 5 TRI 12 11 10 09 08

Contents

To Ella, Daniel and Audrey.

About Right Management

As the world's leading coaching firm, Right Management creates competitive advantage through successful Coaching engagements designed to improve organizational performance through people. ROI-driven, our approach supports leaders and their teams in strategic thinking, business execution, and professional growth in a way that directly impacts financial and organizational performance. By establishing a partnership relationship, Right Management ensures that Coaching links directly to the organization's strategy and other human resource systems. Our proven methodologies and tools have been selected based on rigorous research into what makes the most effective leaders. For large-scale projects, we developed the Coaching Management System – a web-based platform for utilization reports, quality metrics, progress reporting, and ROI measurement. Right Management's business-savvy Coaches are recognized experts in the field of Coaching. In this book, Right Management is pleased to share insights gained from more than 20 years of experience, engaging thousands of leaders and managers in coaching programs from organizations representing all industries and business sectors across the globe.

Right Management is also the premier provider of integrated human capital consulting services and solutions across the employment lifecycle, partnering with organizations to develop and execute innovative solutions for effective implementation of workforce and talent management strategies. Right Management provides customized services and solutions to assess and attract talent, develop talent for emerging leadership roles, identify and develop existing talent, engage employees to ensure alignment with the business strategy, and redeploy and transition employees based on organizational needs. Our success in customizing appropriate solutions for our clients comes from our ability to draw on the expertise of our people, as well as proven processes, methodologies, and tools from any or all of the four areas of the employment lifecycle:

You know that...

... moving your organization forward requires knowing how to find the talent you have and the talent you need

... having the right talent in the right places doing the right things is critical to making the plan, hitting the numbers, and delivering value to your customers

We can help you Attract & Assess the best talent in the marketplace.

You know that...

... developing current and future leadership is a top priority

... unlocking everyone's potential is the best way to beat your competitors, survive, and thrive

We can help you Develop the best people in your industry.

You know that...

... organizational performance depends upon people wanting to give it their best everyday

... people need integrated information and ongoing inspiration to truly transform your business

We can help you Engage & Align your people and your organization.

You know that...

... people who stay after a downsizing remember how you treat the people who leave

... outplacement initiatives need to be orchestrated with skill and dignity

As the world's largest outplacement provider, we can help you orchestrate successful Transition initiatives.

Right Management's core values create a foundation for a high performance culture that enables us to provide the highest quality service to our clients, candidates, stakeholders, and employees, while creating a workplace culture that fosters employee engagement and provides a quality workplace. These values include: commitment and accountability for results; personal growth for our people; treating employees with trust, respect, and candor; sharing information and knowledge company-wide; listening and responding to questions, concerns, and conditions now; bringing together the best resources from around the world to complete a job; thriving on change internally in order to help clients manage change externally; and diversity of people within the company.

More information on Right Management is available at
www.right.com.

Acknowledgments

This book was a joy to research and write since it focused on the subject of talent development and coaching that I have been fortunate enough to work on, and consulted in for most of my career.

I was particularly fortunate to have the help and support of a number of people throughout the research and writing of the book.

I am so grateful to my many colleagues in Right Management who were instrumental in both helping the book come to fruition and in assisting me to get interviews with companies that have a strong tradition of talent management.

I would particularly like to thank the following people: Dominick Volini, Brian Clapp, Endre Lima Lovas, Jack Beighley, Cathy Simpson, Jane Hawkrigg, Arabelle Fedora, Winnie Lanoix, Allan Benowitz, Debra Jackson, Francie Sinnott, Kathy Engstrom, Jennifer McKenzie, Stan Cooper and Concetta Caboy. The people that were interviewed are listed in Appendix 1.

Angela Lonigro, who is a Masters student in Industrial and Organization Psychology at New York University, provided invaluable support by conducting research in topics related to the book and helping the edits to the final draft.

I would also like to thank Michael Erkelenz of Fine Line Writers and Brenda Missen of MIA Communication for their support in creating the manuscript.

As always I thank my family – Brian, Robin and Jeremy, for their support through yet another book.

Finally my thanks goes to Karen Milner, Executive Editor, Professional & Trade Division, John Wiley & Sons Canada, Ltd. for publishing my fourth book.

CHAPTER 1

MVPs and the Talent Crunch

Sports teams are not alone in having their most valuable performers (MVPs). In any organization, about 5 to 10 percent of people in the workforce deliver extraordinary value to the organization – in many cases, two to three times more value than their less gifted colleagues. The MVPs are the people who constantly seek to improve their own performance and that of the organization, who aren't afraid to challenge existing ways of thinking and acting, and who live by the values of the organization and do all they can to achieve its vision. Since their own high performance is never achieved at the expense of their colleagues, they serve as role models for other people, both inside the organization and out. MVPs are team players who seek to develop the skills of their less successful peers, and talent magnets who attract other high-potential individuals from the outside. Everyone wants to work with an MVP. And, of course, managers want to develop and retain their MVPs as effectively as possible. The question is, how?

This question can hardly be said to be new. Wise and successful organizations have always considered talent management a top-priority issue; however, it has assumed a renewed urgency in the last few years. Moreover, that urgency is likely to intensify in the coming years. As never before, talent is, and increasingly will be, in short supply. On one level, it's a simple matter of demographics: the baby boomer generation is retiring and the generations following it lack the numbers to replace it entirely. On another level, it's a matter of development: the world economy is growing and world-class companies are growing with it. As a result, these companies are increasingly talent-hungry, just as the baby boomers start retiring. Not surprisingly, the competition for talent is heating up and the need to retain talent by managing it wisely is becoming an ever higher priority.

Retirement of the Baby Boomers

Managers are fully aware of the trends discussed above and are in many cases, sounding alarm bells themselves. Keith Lawrence, Director of Human Resources at Procter & Gamble Beauty and Healthcare Products notes that his company, "like many companies, particularly in Western Europe and North America," is "facing an increasingly older workforce."

> Over the next three to five years, we stand to lose a number of people to retirement. So we're also trying to get ahead of that a bit by making sure that the bench behind them is as strong as it can be and in capturing their knowledge before they leave.

Debi King, Sr. Vice President of Human Resources, describes a similar situation at MDS Nordion, which began implementing a "talent management strategy about four years ago," because "some of our senior executives in really critical general management roles were aging":

> They had so much knowledge and experience, and yet we had no successors to replace them. The businesses that we're in are so unique that they're not the kind of jobs that you could easily fill from outside the company. We knew that we had better start developing people ourselves or we'd have a big problem. So we started a process to identify people who were considered to have the potential to move into these roles within the next three to five years.

Lawrence and King sound reassuring in their assessments of the challenges facing their respective companies. These organizations appear to have the challenges well in hand.

For an idea of what losing "a number of people" will mean for other organizations – the "many companies, particularly in Western Europe and North America," mentioned by Lawrence – I spoke with Brian Chitester, Vice President of Organization Development and People Capability for PepsiCo International:

I think that, if you look at the baby boom generation hitting retirement, it gets very apparent that for not just us but for most multinational companies, you've got this 5/50 syndrome. In five years 50 percent of your senior managers are going to retire or at least be eligible to do so. That could create a real vacuum in some organizations . . . .

In a recent article in the *Harvard Management Update*, Anne Field calls this impending vacuum "a leadership crisis." She, like Chitester, mentions the 5/50 figure, but notes that it applies to the U.S. in particular. Citing Tamara Erickson, co-author of *Workforce Crisis: How to Beat the Coming Shortage of Skills and Talent* (Harvard Business School Press, 2006), Field observes that retirement rates and the related management vacuum will be even greater in places like Japan, Australia and parts of Europe.[1]

What does it all mean? As Lawrence observes, "It's not easy to develop a senior general manager over night. It takes many years to do that." As if in reply, Tamara Erickson says that companies must "accelerate their leadership development efforts and fast. [They] need to condense and speed up what traditionally has been a fairly lengthy trial-by-fire process."

Company Growth

What company wouldn't cheer on strong growth? The developed economies of the West have been posting solid numbers year in and year out. Many economies in the developing world are expanding at break-neck speed. The so-called BRIC nations (Brazil, Russia, India and China) are quickly emerging as new global economic powerhouses. Enterprises with the resources and knowledge to compete on continental and global scales are growing by leaps and bounds. You might be thinking they're ready to throw a party or go on parade. Yet behind every silver lining lurks a dark cloud.

The very success of these global champions only threatens to deepen the impending talent crisis. As Keith Lawrence of Procter & Gamble explains, "One of our biggest issues is having sufficient talent to meet our business needs, particularly in the developing markets. It

---

1 Anne Field, "When the Boomers Leave, Will Your Company Have the Leaders It Needs?" *Harvard Management Update: A Newsletter from Harvard Business School,* Vol.12, no. 4 (April 2007), p.10.

isn't the lack of ideas or lack of technologies. It's just that we do not have a sufficient pipeline of talent to meet the tremendous growth in our business." Astonishingly, Brian Chitester regards company growth as potentially a bigger contributor to the battle for talent than demographics and the remarkable "5/50 syndrome" he mentioned earlier in our interview: "I'd say the biggest component of all that is affecting our need for talent is simply the growth of the company. We are growing tremendously and, even if nobody leaves, we will need talented people to lead this growing business."

For some companies, "now" is already too late. Bob Hedley, Corporate Vice President of Leadership and Human Resource Management Systems for Canada's Maple Leaf Foods, relates that a talent shortage has already adversely affected the company's plans for continuing growth:

> About four years ago we passed up a major acquisition outside Canada because we felt we didn't have the talent to pull it off. It was not because we didn't have the money or the knowledge but because we didn't have the depth of leadership talent. We would have had to move people who were in critical jobs in Canada to the United States in order to do it and we just did not have sufficient talent. We know that we won't be able to achieve our growth plans unless we have more depth and high-potential talent.

Clearly, Maple Leaf Foods has been (and is) a very successful company. Four years ago, they had grown to the point where they had the resources and knowledge to make a major acquisition. Only a shortage of "high-potential talent" stopped them. It's a shortage they continue to address to this day.

One potential answer to the evolving talent shortage might be to fill positions by looking further afield. This response, however, brings its own challenges. David Denison, President and CEO of the Canada Pension Plan Investment Board (CPP Investment Board), presides over an organization "that is growing rapidly . . . into new areas of investment and into new geographies." As a result, the CPP Investment Board is "now hiring people in Hong Kong and in London." But, says Denison, "identifying people in those markets who are both the high-potential talent and also a cultural fit within the organization is a particular challenge. The people dimension will be absolutely the single biggest factor in our success over the next few years. How do we get the right people into this organization and how do we get them aligned with our strategy and our culture and how do we make them effective?" For fast-growing organizations like the CPP Investment Board, simply hiring talent in places where they are newly active may not prove to be the quick fix it seems at first. Cultural issues add a layer of complexity to the situation and inevitably slow the development of talent. Acculturation takes time.

The Competition for Talent

If some organizations are already feeling the effects of the talent crunch, it is little wonder that the competition for attracting and re-taining talent is showing signs of heating up. In fact, according to Pep-siCo International's Brian Chitester, "the war for talent is going to heat up like never before," and Pepsi is already strengthening its defenses: "It's in our best interest to let our people know that we're concerned about them and that they can have a career here. We are committed to doing that by creating a career growth model for everybody and by giving extra attention to those who can get to the senior-most levels in the company."

Use it or lose it is the new imperative driving talent management. Many organizations know full well that their talented people have many suitors. Talent must be developed or it will be enticed elsewhere. Mark Bornemann, Vice President of Human Resources and Risk, describes the situation at LoJack Corporation: "We want to keep our A players. If they're not engaged or challenged here, they are going to become engaged and challenged at our competitor company, and we certainly don't want that." According to Meg Jones, Senior Vice President for Human Resources and Chief Learning Officer at The Children's Hospital of Philadelphia, "Leaders are in short supply. We're a leading organization, and we know that a differentiator for us has been our people and our leaders of people, and will continue to be. We know that our leaders and high performers get calls from headhunters every week. We're a big pond that people like to fish in; so we've got to continue developing our talent here for the sake of the hospital as well as of the individuals involved – to help them see that there's an investment in them and that this is a place where they can grow and develop and achieve new heights in terms of their own career."

David Denison of the CPP Investment Board expresses the perspective of the buyers in the same market: "Across the world there just aren't a lot of experienced people with the kind of background that we need in infrastructure investment, and when we look in Canada, there are virtually none. So we have to be able to attract these people from wherever they may be working. We have recently hired someone from Australia and have had to relocate him. The specialized skill sets we're looking for are in high demand across the world; so there's a really serious battle to attract these people." Some organizations simply don't have the internal base from which to develop their own talent. They have no choice but to look outside the organization, and they are prepared to scour the globe to fill their needs.

Retaining Talent—An Ever Higher Priority

With the competition for talent heating up, the success of organizations in the marketplace will increasingly depend on their success on the human resources front. As more people retire and as organizations continue to expand into new areas of business and into new geographies, continuing prosperity will depend on managing talent wisely – in short, on developing and, above all, retaining talent.

The corporate world is aware of this priority. "We don't want to be in the 'Oh no, what do we do now?' mode," says Mark Bornemann of LoJack. "So we want to be prepared to have these people groomed and ready to move up, and this also increases their engagement. I am a true believer that great employees only work for great companies." Teri Kozikowski, Vice President of Global Organization, Staffing and Development at GE Real Estate, similarly emphasizes the importance of retention: "We have to make sure that we're retaining our great employees. We run pretty lean here and losing somebody hurts from many standpoints."

For Denise Lockaby, Director of Professional Development at The Stride Rite Corporation, retention is of particular importance in different functional areas and niches: "The first primary goal is to develop bench strength for our senior management, and that's on the high-potential side. We have to make sure that we are building and not buying our top talent." But the focus at The Stride Rite Corporation is not just on managerial expertise: "We also need to retain our high-value associates because they might go somewhere else. These high-value individuals are usually people who have a very specific technical skill that is needed in the market. They might be a design director or they might be somebody who is a product developer, somebody who really understands how a shoe gets put together and all of the manufacturing processes around that. They are fabulous at it and we want to keep them."

In many organizations, the need to retain talent translates into a need to retain specific skills. Paul Mayer of Altana echoes Denise Lockaby: "Many of our people have been with us for a number of years. They've proven their worth and they have a genuine skill set that is very important to the organization. We don't have that many layers of management so we really like to keep these people as involved or engaged in their job as they possibly can be. We do that by showing them that we're really willing to invest in their future and by giving them opportunities within the organization. They do not have to leave the company and find this type of growth and challenge at another company." In a tightening talent market, people with specialized technical skills are more in demand than ever. Organizations know that they have to do everything they can to keep them.

Retaining the MVP

Standing at the pinnacle of the talent pyramid, MVPs are the people that organizations most wish to attract and retain. As Bill Roiter and I show at length in our jointly authored book, *Corporate MVPs: Managing Your Company's Most Valuable Performers*,[2] MVPs deliver extraordinary results. They redefine their jobs to take themselves and their team to the next level. They focus on what they can do not for themselves but for the team and the organization as a whole. Knowing how to read cultures well, they succeed anywhere in the organization and in any geography and culture. They are, in other words, precisely the sort of people most valued by organizations such as David Denison's CCP Investment Board – large global players striving to adapt to rapid growth in their businesses. As the impending talent crunch unfolds, MVPs will be more in demand than ever.

As Bill and I found in *Corporate MVPs*, good management is the key to success in both attracting and retaining these high-value performers. MVPs require not special treatment but *thoughtful* treatment. MVPs want to see their contributions valued. They feel a powerful commitment to the organization and like to be involved in a broad

---

2 Margaret Butteriss and Bill Roiter, *Corporate MVPs: Managing Your Company's Most Valuable Performers*, John Wiley & Sons, Ltd., 2004.

capacity. So, managers are well advised to solicit ideas from MVPs. They've usually got them and are eager to share them. MVPs also want to receive recognition for their worth – in terms of both compensation and frequent feedback. We found that MVPs see compensation as a measure of their value. It is one of the benchmarks they use to judge how highly the organization values their contributions and their potential.

More than anything else, what matters in managing MVPs successfully is to provide them with opportunities for career development and for challenge. Managers must know what their MVPs are looking for in their current job and where they want their careers to go in the future. On the basis of that knowledge, they must supply MVPs with frequent feedback and involve them in tailored development programs. Managers must also provide these people with challenges; otherwise they will get bored and leave. In other words, create and maintain a culture around MVPs that enables them to be productive and motivated. Make sure that they have a clear view of the company strategy and that the results they and their teams are expected to achieve are consistent with this strategy. Ensure also that your management style allows the MVP to produce outstanding results and to grow professionally. Such a style involves delegating key responsibilities to the MVP and avoids micro-managing him or her.

MVPs need to keep growing and learning. Mismanaging them may cause them to leave and go to competitors – a thought that can cause business leaders and HR executives to have sleepless nights! As we said in *Corporate MVPs*, "One of the key roles of any leader is to ensure that a talent pool exists to fulfill the succession needs of the organization. This will prevent the dependence of the organization on the leader and a few MVPs whose departure would be disastrous for the future success of the business. The manager, therefore, needs to coach the current MVPs on how to ensure their own success, and also on how to develop and strengthen other potential MVPs in order to ensure that there is a vibrant talent pool."

Reasons for Writing this Book

As we have seen, the question of how to retain talent, especially MVPs, the most talented of the talented, is becoming more pressing in a world facing a talent crisis. Building on the foundations laid by

Corporate MVPs, a wide-ranging look at the MVP, this book narrows the focus to the key issue of retention. More specifically, it focuses on retaining MVPs through development and, above all, coaching. What are the development needs of MVPs and how does coaching fit in? How is coaching the MVP different from coaching others? How do you choose a coach? What is the role of management and HR in working with coaches and MVPs? These are among the questions this book addresses in an attempt to create a route map to successfully retaining the MVP.

Since the focus of this book is development, its scope extends beyond MVPs themselves to consider another type of talent – high-potential employees. These are employees who are already high performers but who also have the potential to reach more senior positions and possibly achieve MVP status. Developing these talented performers, no less than developing MVPs, is a crucial task in the emerging talent-short world. In developing these high-potentials, the same questions apply.

In answering these questions and drawing up my map, I have relied on research into the experiences and best practices of major organizations with robust leadership development programs. My research consisted of a large number of interviews with managers intimately involved in their organizations' talent retention processes. I wanted to find out how various companies thought about identifying their MVPs and what they did to develop them. I particularly wanted to know what role coaching played in that development. To this end, I also interviewed a number of coaches. The results of all these interviews provide the support for the conclusions I reach.

In total, 39 people were interviewed and we will hear the thoughts they expressed in these interviews throughout the book. The companies interviewed are listed on the following page. Further details on these companies and on the interviewees themselves are provided in Appendix 1.

The book consists of ten chapters that provide a comprehensive look at developing the MVP. Chapter 2 offers a general overview of the culture and framework that must be created if effective development is to take place. Chapter 3 considers means of assessing MVPs as a first step in creating a development plan. Chapters 4 to 9, the heart of the book, address coaching – when to use it, how to approach it, how to find a coach, and how HR and management should be involved. The final chapter, Chapter 10, examines the benefits of coaching and development and the challenges and methods of measuring return on investment.

Alpha Trading Systems

Atlanta

Canada Pension Plan Investment Board

Chubb Group of Insurance Companies

CSL Behring

Fidelity Investments

GE Real Estate

Leadership Futures

LoJack Corporation

Maple Leaf Foods

McGraw Hill

MDS Inc. and MDS Nordion

Merck & Co.

Millipore Corporation

PepsiCo International

Procter & Gamble

Raytheon

Right Management

Rogers Communications

Schering-Plough

Scotiabank

Shell International

State Street Corporation

The Children's Hospital of Philadelphia

The Stride Rite Corporation

UBS Financial Services and UBS Investment Bank

CHAPTER 2

Creating the Culture and Framework for Talent Management

Successful companies understand that they can't develop their talent in a vacuum. As executives like PepsiCo International's Brian Chitester know all too well, the growth of the business very often depends on having the right kind of talent, with appropriate competencies and experience, in the organization. Recognizing the importance of their MVPs in growing the business, companies are increasingly treating talent management and leadership development as an integral part of their business strategy and planning. It cannot simply be left to the Human Resources department to come up with some specialized training programs: such a practice will be doomed to failure. Talent management has to be an integral part of the key business processes, with all managers and key senior personnel on board.

My interviews with many senior executives for this book, in tandem with my own experience as a Human Resource executive, consultant, and coach, have shown me that a company's success in identifying and developing high-performing and high-potential talent depends on three key components:

1. CEO Commitment
2. Development of a philosophy/framework
3. Implementation of the framework across the entire organization.

Number one is the commitment of the CEO and the senior leadership to developing talent. It is senior management that creates the culture to encourage the development of talent. In the research paper "How Top 20 Companies Grow Great Leaders," Hewitt Associates found that CEOs and boards of directors in the Top 20 Companies "are actively engaged in leadership development programs and personally involved in the selection, review and development of their best talent."[1] CEOs also often act as role models and actively support the coaching of MVPs. Their role in the process is therefore of paramount importance. Second is having a strategy in place – a clearly defined philosophy and framework – to identify and develop talent. Third, and closely related, is implementing the framework across the whole organization. It is the CEO who is often relied upon to champion the process and ensure that the framework is implemented consistently throughout the organization – again underlining the importance of the CEO's commitment.

CEO and Senior Management Commitment

A number of the senior executives I interviewed for this book spoke from experience about how integral the commitment of the CEO is to managing and developing talent. Vas Nair, Vice President and Chief Learning Officer at Schering-Plough Corporation, emphasizes the importance of the CEO's commitment to implementing a clear business strategy. "In April, 2003, Fred Hassan joined as CEO of Schering-Plough, and he along with the leadership team developed a concrete five-step strategy for the next six to eight years. This strategy gave direction and clarity about what the leadership team expected in terms of priorities and subsequently, our 'people' programs. It provided me the focus required to create a strong foundation for performance management, talent development, and a culture targeted towards learning."

Keith Lawrence, Director of Human Resources of Procter & Gamble's Beauty and Healthcare Products, looks at the issue of CEO commitment from the perspective of developing the next generation of leaders for the organization. "A huge part of the jobs of our CEO and senior management team is to build in the next generation of P&G talent. Their support is founded on the belief that at P&G our brands and our people are our most valuable assets." At P&G, additional incentive exists: "Much of our personal wealth is dependent upon the

---

1 Hewitt Associates, "How Top 20 Companies Grow Great Leaders," 2005, p. 2. www.hewittassociates.com

continued success of P&G. So we all have a vested interest in ensuring that the stock does well by developing the next generation of leaders who will make this happen."

One reason the CEO's involvement is so important is that there is no *one* stock formula for developing a successful leader. In today's global marketplace, business success depends on the CEO's ability to develop leadership that is appropriate in different markets. This means ensuring that leadership and management reflect the diversity of customers and employees in different parts of the world. At State Street Corporation, the goal of the global talent management program is to reflect diversity in its senior positions. Wendy Watson, Executive Vice President of Global Services, explains: "When Ron Logue became CEO, the majority of our revenue came out of the U.S. He set a target that we become a truly global company, and he wanted 50 percent of our revenue to come from outside the U.S. He also set some pretty strong goals in terms of diversity to ensure that our leadership and management reflected the diversity of our geographies and customer base. He wanted to increase the number of women, people of color and non-U.S. passport holders in senior positions. One of his goals is to bridge that gap over a three-year period. So the goal of the talent management program is to identify those people in the organization and to see whether we should be doing something to accelerate them and place them in more senior positions."

As part of the strategy, the company brings people from its offices in Asia and Europe to work for a few years at the Boston office so that they receive broader development, and then sends them back to their home offices to take on higher and broader positions.

In short, senior executive commitment is key to future employee success. Research backs up this finding, but, as a Corporate Leadership Council study notes, "we still have a long way to go in getting that commitment. When senior executives commit to employee development and act on those commitments, employees' likelihood of success in more senior, critical roles increases about 30 percent. However, just 16 percent of employees report their organization effectively and consistently communicates executives' dedication to the development of employees."[2]

Without future employee success, where will your company be in ten to twenty years? As Brian Chitester says, "At PepsiCo International

2 Corporate Executive Board, Corporate Leadership Council, "Improving Talent Management Outcomes: 10 Talent Management Insights for the Chief Human Resources Officer." *Chief Human Resources Officer Briefing*, 2007, p. 19.

we say that the people side of the equation is just as important as driving the business. It's not just *what* results you produce but *how* you're getting your results, through people. Let's face it, when you are a senior person in the company, we don't need you to prove technical prowess anymore. That's what got you there. We now need you to develop the talent so that they can continue to drive the business into the future."

CEO as Role Model

CEOs and senior leaders not only set the direction for talent manage-ment as part of their business strategy, they also act as role models for the kind of leadership they are looking for. As the Corporate Leadership Council study notes, "Senior executives acting as good role models for developing employees is the single most important factor for driving leadership quality. Excellence here increases an organization's prob-ability of being a top-tier leadership organization by 84.1 percent."[3]

But how do you know if you are being a good role model? Assessing your own performance is one way, of course, but it elicits only one perspective – your own. It is important to get the views of others and this often provokes a strong motivation to effect change. In recent years, management development has increasingly involved this kind of "360-degree" feedback – ratings of performance from peers, superiors and subordinates (all in anonymous form).

This is the premise behind the Awareness Program for Executive Excellence (APEX). APEX is an enhanced 360-degree feedback experi-ence created specifically to help senior-level executives meet the chal-lenge of providing leadership at the highest levels of management. Executives who go through APEX receive feedback from sources such as personal interviews; observations from friends and family mem-bers; psychometric measures of personality, motivation, and needs; a personal and family biographical inventory; and reports of team performance and satisfaction, among others. (For more details about APEX, see Appendix 2.)

The senior executives of two Canadian organizations, Maple Leaf Foods and the Canada Pension Plan Investment Board, are using 360-degree feedback, including the APEX model, not only to receive feedback for their potential leaders but also to be good role models

---

3 Corporate Leadership Council, 2007, p. 18.

by using it themselves first. "I go through the 360-process myself and then roll it out to other team members," says Canada Pension Plan Investment Board President and CEO David Denison. "My strong belief is that leaders have to go through it themselves – they have to live through an experience that convinces them that there is value and meaning in it for them before doing the same thing for their direct reports." In turn, Denison expects his direct reports to be a similar role model for their teams as they and then their teams go through the feedback process. In this way, the CEO's commitment to being a role model for leadership filters down through the entire organization.

Maple Leaf Foods CEO Michael McCain has gone through the APEX model twice, in 1998 and 2005, in order to follow through on his commitment to creating and implementing a personal development plan for the company based on this kind of 360-degree feedback. The company now uses APEX two to three times per year for its top potential executives. "When we see somebody who we think has truly got presidential potential and they're near ready to fill these positions, then we make APEX available to them and give them really deep feedback," says Bob Hedley, the company's Corporate Vice President of Leadership and Human Resource Management Systems. "When your team and your Board see a CEO who does this and then invests in other high-potential people, they are very impressed and they buy into it." In effect, both CEOs have put their money where their mouths are. As Denison says, if the leaders themselves don't go through a particular experience or process, "it just becomes a rote exercise that has some value but not deep value."

CEO's Support for Coaching

Actively supporting coaching is another important component of the commitment CEOs can make to developing their talent. "Coaching" has sometimes been given the negative connotation of being needed when a person is having difficulties in, or even failing in, their job. Meg Jones "brought coaching out of the closet," as she puts it, when she became Senior Vice President for Human Resources and Chief Learning Officer at The Children's Hospital of Philadelphia. "Before I arrived, coaching was pretty much *persona non grata*. There were people who had been getting coaching but it was a very hush-hush kind of thing because the perspective was that if you had a coach you must have one foot on a banana peel and the other foot in mid-air."

But Jones was a big proponent of coaching, having been coached in her previous positions and also having a coach in her first three months at the hospital, which considerably eased a difficult transition. "I went to our CEO and suggested that every new executive to the organization have the opportunity for a coach, and he agreed." With the CEO's support, the introduction of coaching has been so successful at the hospital that the managers of people who are coming into the organization are now *asking* for coaches for their new leaders.

CEO support for coaching was also a key factor in getting coaching accepted at LoJack Corporation – the global leader in stolen vehicle recovery systems. Mark Bornemann, Vice President of Human Resources and Risk, introduced coaching to LoJack six or seven years ago, but was aware that management didn't necessarily see the value in the coaching process – until a new CEO arrived. "During his first week with the company, I solicited his support and identified a few people I thought would certainly benefit from coaching, and in a couple of weeks there was top down support for coaching."

As it turns out, the new CEO was also a big proponent of coaching – because, like Meg Jones, he had been coached himself in a previous position (as president of the North American division of a large organization). "I certainly saw the value in how it helped him personally," says Bornemann, "and saw that as an opportunity to try the same thing with other executives and middle managers who had high potential."

Creating the Philosophy and Integrated Talent Management Framework

As we have seen, the commitment of the CEO is integral to talent management, but that commitment is like a boat floating aimlessly on the ocean if it is not anchored to a particular philosophy and framework. Creating a philosophy and an integrated talent management framework is a key requirement for an organization setting out to develop its talent and leadership. The framework makes possible the consistent identification of talent across the organization and a consistent and integrated approach to the development of that talent.

This framework is often created by the Human Resources function, but it must be on behalf of, and under the guidance of, the senior leadership team. Managers need to have a clear idea of what is expected of them in terms of developing their employees. They need clear templates and guides as to how to implement the process. As Vas Nair of Schering-Plough pointed out above, having a set of steps laid out by the CEO and senior management gave her "direction and clarity" about what the leadership team expected in terms of priorities so she could create and implement talent development programs that met the Company's business objectives.

The goal at Procter & Gamble is to have everyone contributing at their full potential. Keith Lawrence explains that an integrated system of performance expectations, feedback, and performance reviews is used in the company to ensure that everyone is doing their job and receiving the help they need to succeed and perform at their peak. "We try to ensure that managers are giving clear feedback to their employees and making training available to them. We ensure that new hires get frequent performance reviews – every three to six months. There are very rigorous checks in place to make sure that feedback and training are happening for all employees, particularly for our top talent."

The philosophy behind this rigorous framework? "You are not going to be successful if you just deliver business results. You also need to grow your organization, and that means giving special attention to your top talent so that they reach their full potential."

Building a stronger team is also the philosophy underpinning the framework in place at MDS Inc. The company has four core processes, one of which is talent management. "Our direction to our managers, over and above delivering on their performance commitments, is, very simply, to build a team that is stronger in six months than it is today," says MDS Inc.'s Executive Vice President of Global Human Resources Jim Reid. "It's very clear, from the moment you join the company, that our goal is to make one of your signature qualities the ability to make the right people decisions."

Consistent Global Approach

Creating the framework for talent management for a company with a *global* focus presents a particular challenge due to the sheer scope of the task at hand. Science-based health care company Schering-Plough has spent four years building a global infrastructure for its processes, systems, and communications, including its HR programs and policies. Vas Nair explains how the company created the framework for talent management to be consistent with its new global infrastructure.

- We defined the culture for the company and articulated what we expected of our people. This involved the creation of six Leader Behaviors that formed the foundation and helped us shape our high-performing culture: cross-functional team work and collaboration, shared accountability and, transparency, listening and learning, benchmarking and continuously improving coaching and developing others and business integrity. The Leader Behaviors were rolled out worldwide and contribute significantly to how we work at Schering-Plough.

- Every colleague is expected to be a role model and to demonstrate the six Leader Behaviors, and everyone is held accountable to the Leader Behaviors.

- The Leader Behaviors were incorporated into the global performance management program, which in turn influences the reward system. Worldwide, our colleagues are very clear on how the Leader Behaviors impact their performance.

- Development planning was plugged into our performance management program, which not only supports a colleague's performance objectives, but includes the Leader Behaviors.

- We subsequently built the global talent management program on the foundation of the performance management program. We defined "top talent" at Schering-Plough – which includes the dimensions of "high performer" and "high potential". Also incorporated into the talent management process is very explicit roles and responsibilities of the colleague, manager, and next-level manager.

- The next order of business was creating a global behavioral competency framework. Here, our colleagues have access to the library of skills and attributes required to be successful in a given position.

Creation of Competency Framework

As Nair says in her last point above, part of creating a global talent framework is defining the required competencies that need to be displayed across the organization. Simply put, such competencies are the areas in which colleagues need to excel if they are to achieve their performance objectives and, subsequently, the business strategy. In order to define the required competencies, a company needs to know what its corporate strategy is going to be for the next three or five years. If the strategy changes, the competency framework should evolve to align with this change.

Raytheon has created a three-tiered competency model aiming at painting a picture of the executive that the company will need for 2010. "Now that we have a picture of what that executive looks like and what skills, behaviors, and experiences he or she should have been through or exhibited, we have started to align our development programs to that picture," says Raytheon's Daniel Sonsino, Senior Manager of Talent Management and Succession Planning. "Since we understand where our corporate strategy is going, we can reflect on what our corporate leadership should look like and then target specific development programs for them."

Raytheon's leadership competency model supports its executives, middle managers and front-line management. This competency model describes a consistent set of behaviors that are specific to the different roles in the organization. "For instance," says Sonsino, "when it comes to strategy development and implementation, we expect our executives to exhibit different behaviors than our front-line leaders. But we do want consistency of approach for strategic thinking as a competency."

Raytheon's senior executives understand the importance of applying consistency to its approach. Says Sonsino: "Our competency model is essentially at the hub of our talent management model. All of the company programs are designed from or based on the leadership competency model, so that there is program consistency throughout the organization."

Identification of Potential

So you have identified your corporate strategy for the next five or ten years, you have reflected on what your corporate leadership should look like to meet that future need, and you have targeted specific development programs for that leadership. Now, how do you identify the specific potential that exists in your organization to take on those leadership roles?

Some of the companies I interviewed not only define the leadership competencies that they expect of all leaders but have also spent time defining the characteristics they look for in an individual who has the potential to move to positions with broader responsibilities or to higher positions in the organization.

Two companies that I interviewed use the Corporate Leadership Council (CLC) approach to identify potential. (I will discuss this approach more fully in Chapter 3.) The CLC characteristics of potential are:

- Aspiration
- Engagement
- Ability

As one of the people interviewed noted, "We then look further at a person's learning agility and openness to learning more about themselves and about the business. We have created a new leadership model based on some of these factors. One of our key focuses is innovation."

Shell International also uses three indicators to assess potential. These are:

- Capacity
- Achievement
- Relationships

GE Real Estate takes a slightly different approach to identifying potential. Its process starts with employees self-assessing their performance during the previous year, which are reviewed first by the manager and then their HR Manager, who provide their assessments of the employee, including performance, strengths, development needs and career interests. Ultimately all employee performance write-ups are reviewed by the CEO.

"We take a look at the entire employee population and determine where each employee falls in terms of performance and potential," explains GE Real Estate's VP of Global Organization, Staffing and Development, Teri Kozikowski. "We then take a deeper look at people who are seen to have achieved great performance and see how they demonstrate the GE core values – Imagine, Solve, Build, and Lead. We also take a look to see if these people have the five growth traits that we identified four or five years ago as key to successful leaders – External Focus, Clear Thinker, Imagination, Inclusiveness, and Expertise. We believe that the people who have demonstrated the growth traits as key to successful leaders will be able to drive continuous growth in the company and continue to personally excel.

"What we want is someone who not only can think about the next big idea and try to see things from different perspectives, but who also has the courage to take a stand and push those things through or make the tough call and stop a project. It's these growth traits that really help differentiate people from the rest of the pack."

Consistent Implementation of Framework Across the Organization

A key part of an effective talent development strategy is, as Teri Kozikowski says above, taking a look at "the entire employee population." In other words, for the framework to work, it has to be implemented across the entire organization – and it has to be implemented in a consistent way. The Hewitt study found that the Top 20 Companies in 2005 have a clear focus on the "consistent execution" of their leadership practices. "The Top 20 Companies find that this focus on execution allows them to better identify more great talent within their organizations, as well as to attract the best talent from outside the organization."[4]

But how do you convince your senior personnel and managers to take a consistent, organization-wide approach to developing talent? I know from my own experience that many leaders and managers like to do performance management and talent assessment and management in the ways they have always done it. They consider their business

4 Hewitt, 2005, p. 3.

situation to be unique and to require a business- or function-specific process. But each manager following his or her own practices leads to a haphazard approach to identifying and developing talent, which ultimately doesn't serve the organization.

Once again, many organizations rely on their CEO to champion the process and to play a major role in it. Says Jim Reid of MDS: "The CEO reviews people four levels down in terms of development planning. We do these reviews every six months, and they are very thorough. We plot every team. From the CEO, we go down four levels, and then he looks at the results. We then go deeper down the organization from there."

Similarly the CEO of Procter & Gamble does a rigorous annual employee review, which, as Keith Lawrence explains, ensures consistency. "It's a very rigorous review to make sure that all of the elements of successful development are in place. So that's really the check process for the high-potential folks, and it ensures that we follow a consistent process." At Raytheon, the CEO personally leads the annual HR review process. "He travels to each business and completes reviews with each business or function," says Daniel Sonsino. "We really couldn't be this successful without having his complete support, drive, and sponsorship."

Management Accountability and Reinforcement for Talent Management

Of course, the roll-out of the global talent management program cannot be based solely on CEO commitment and support. Managers have to be given the appropriate tools and skills. They also need some reinforcement to ensure that these tools and processes are being implemented, consistently, across the organization. This reinforcement is often in the form of compensation. There's nothing like influencing the pocketbook or wallet as a means to get the program started. Compensation goes hand in hand with accountability. The Hewitt study notes that in addition to consistent execution of leadership practices, the Top 20 Companies in 2005 also have a clear focus on accountability. "The Top 20 Companies formally hold their leaders accountable for the success of leadership programs, the development of their employees, and the development of their own leadership capabilities.

Leaders are held accountable for these results through their annual incentive, with up to 20 percent or more of incentive pay impacted by these behaviors."[5]

PepsiCo International is one company that holds its leaders accountable through incentives. "We make sure that we review how well managers do in terms of developing talent and coaching their folks," explains Brian Chitester. "We also ensure that they consider diversity and leveraging differences in their development plans. All of these factors go into the 50 percent of your increase that relates to people management. This all affects not just your increase and your bonus but also your long-term stock options."

Challenges to Implementing Talent Management and Leadership Development Programs

Implementing a consistent, organization-wide talent management process is not without its challenges. I have found that there are two main challenges:

1. Convincing managers (and employees) to accept the concept of corporate property
2. Ensuring consistency in rating particular groups of employees.

The Concept of Corporate Property

A few years ago, the key members of the HR team I was part of held a meeting with the senior executives of the organization on the topic of talent management. All of the executives who were responsible for a large business unit or key function agreed that they would allow their key performers and high-potential employees to be part of a corporate talent pool. The people in the pool could then be assigned to different roles in the organization in order to further their development and prepare them for bigger roles. After this decision was made, there was a break in the meeting. Outside the conference room, I saw two executives having a discussion. And then I overheard one say to the

---

5 Hewitt, 2005, p. 3.

other: "I will let you have John ---- for your new position, as long as you give me Tom ----."

What's wrong with this picture? In the meeting, these same executives had agreed to the concept of a "corporate talent pool," which presupposes that the key performers and high-potential employees are "owned" by the company, not by a particular business unit or function – that is, they are "corporate property." In the meeting, the executives had agreed to allow their top performers to be available for assignments and job opportunities anywhere in the company, as long as it was seen as part of their long-term development plan. But during the break, the two executives resorted to the old "horse-trading process." In doing so, they were expressing a fear, common to many leaders, that if they give up their key players, they won't necessarily be replaced by others with the same qualities and drive for success, and this will put the success and results of their team in jeopardy. Even if the replacements do have the required qualities, many managers believe it will take a long time to bring them up to speed and get them used to working on the new team.

State Street's Wendy Watson sums up the reluctance of some managers to buy into the concept of corporate property: "Many people think that identifying your top talent is a bad thing to do because then you're probably going to be asked to give them up and let them take on another career opportunity. Then you don't know who you're going to get as a replacement."

What these managers are forgetting is that the success or results of their particular team will mean nothing if the organization as a whole is suffering. Allowing high-potential employees to take on different roles and positions in the organization to further their skills and experience may one day produce a new CEO who takes the company to new heights. The whole, as they say, is greater than the sum of its parts.

Brian Chitester of PepsiCo International describes the reluctance to accept the concept of corporate property as a "three-legged stool": "One manager says 'I don't want to give up the talent I've been building,' and the other manager says 'I don't want to accept the talent I don't know,' and then there's the person being discussed who doesn't want to move in the first place."

That third leg of the stool – the employee's own reluctance to move – often, Chitester says, stems from older, long-time employees who have the mental model that says, "I don't have to move to grow." "You have to start seeding the idea with the employee early on that they have to move to new positions and take on new challenges if they want to succeed," Chitester advises.

Consistency of Rating Employees

The second main challenge to implementing an organization-wide, consistently applied framework for developing talent is to make sure you are including *all* your employees, and not neglecting certain groups. Royal Dutch Shell identified three areas that needed to be improved in the area of high potential assessment. These areas – which are by no means unique to Shell – were the rating of women, staff in Asia, and technical staff. They also found a reluctance to identify high potential early with the possible result of losing some of the very best early on in their career.

They found that both women and staff in Asia tend to have lower indicated potential than the general population of staff and that the process for assessing them is sometimes less reliable, or simply not completed. "This in spite of the fact that half of our graduates in commercial disciplines are women and that 30 percent of our technical recruits are women and that we are growing our business significantly in Asia," says Shell's M.J. Conway. Conway notes that at Shell, mobility is an important factor in realizing high potential and perhaps women are perceived to be less mobile than their male counterparts. "So we're now going to pay particular attention to women in the process for potential assessment." As for the third group, technical staff, Conway notes that such staff has slightly lower indicated potential in the system than commercial staff. "We can see that our technical staff progress more slowly through the grades than staff in commercial disciplines such as finance or HR. The progression of engineers and scientists is particularly well organized and rigorous against professional standards. The stage gates are robust and yet we have to also ensure that we have a positive view of longer term potential and progress the very best quickly through the organization." Shell's awareness of, and plans to improve, the inconsistencies in its process for developing talent constitute a valuable example for all companies who are looking to create an effective talent management culture and framework.

Checklist for Creating a Talent Management Culture and Framework

❏ Make sure your CEO and senior management are committed to developing talent. Are they:
- Acting as role models?
- Actively supporting employee coaching?
- Taking the lead in the performance review process?

❏ Develop a company philosophy and framework to anchor your talent management program.

❏ Ensure there is consistency in the application of your talent management program by giving managers specific templates, tools, guides, and processes for identifying and developing talent.

❏ Hold your managers accountable for the successes of their programs by rewarding their successes with pay raises and bonuses.

❏ Do you know what your corporate strategy is for the next five or ten years? Once you do, you can develop a picture of what leadership competencies you will need and target your programs at developing the kind of leadership you need.

❏ Encourage your managers to buy into the concept of "corporate property," whereby employees are given the opportunity to take on different positions and roles in the organization to further their development, which will ultimately benefit the organization as a whole.

❏ Are you applying your talent management program across the whole organization, including women, ethnic groups, and overlooked technical staff?

CHAPTER 3

The Use of Assessment Approaches and Tools to Identify and Develop Talent

Identifying and developing their future leaders is not something successful companies treat in a haphazard way. Assessments are increasingly being used to identify MVPs, as well as those who have the potential to become MVPs. Assessments also play an important role in creating a development plan for MVPs so they continue to grow and be challenged – and stay with your company. And just as talent management and leadership development have become an integral part of business processes, so the approaches to the assessment of talent itself have become much more rigorous. In my interviews, I discovered that companies are very aware of the need to assess their talent and are doing so in a methodical way. The companies I interviewed are employing a wide range of assessment tools, from custom designed to commercially available, not only to identify their high-potential employees but also to develop appropriate plans and coaching for them. Some rank their talent against various grids and measurements. Some make use of assessment review sessions, and/or bring in experts, while still others put their potential candidates through an assessment center process. Some begin their assessments right at the hiring stage. Whatever approaches organizations are using, the goal is the same: to identify and confirm their MVPs and then groom them for future leadership roles within the company.

In this chapter we will examine the different approaches companies take to assessment, and the different tools they use, for three purposes:

1. To identify MVPs
2. To create development plans
3. To assist in the coaching process

Assessment for Identifying MVPs

Assessments play a key role in the identification of MVPs during the hiring process, as part of job performance and as a part of talent reviews.

Assessment as Part of the Hiring Process

Some companies begin their assessment of potential talent even before an individual has come on board, that is, during the job interview process. This is especially true when organizations are hiring at the managerial level, as I discovered in my interviews with the Canadian Pension Plan Investment Board and MDS Inc. Says the CPP Investment Board's David Denison: "Assessment starts from the moment we do the hiring. As a developing, evolving organization, when we recruit for such positions as the head of infrastructure investing, we are by definition looking for that high-potential person to fill that role."

MDS uses various assessment approaches during its hiring process, including cognitive tests administered by a trained organizational psychologist, followed by structured interviews and interactive testing. "What we're trying to do," explains Executive Vice President of Global Human Resources Jim Reid, "is select out the cream of the crop, so that from day one you know what the individual is bringing to the table and what their longer-term potential might be."

Job Performance as an Approach to Assessment

Of course, it's not always possible to assess high potential at the initial interview stage. Job performance clearly remains one of the key indicators for identifying, or confirming, whether or not a person can be considered a MVP or high-potential employee. Evaluating job performance reveals the results employees are producing, as well as their approach to their work. "Once we've hired someone into the organization," says Denison, "we can determine if we have someone who's a self-starter and who can see beyond the work that we're putting on his or her desk. If they say, 'I see a need, I see an opportunity here, let me run with that,' that's our first signal that they are a potential MVP."

A key element of job performance that several companies pointed to as an indicator of high potential is learning agility – a person's willingness to learn and to keep learning. Learning agility often translates into the ability to learn in totally new roles and in very different organizations – something crucial in a person you're grooming for a leadership role. PepsiCo International is one company that has built an assessment for learning agility into its new leadership model. "Through this kind of assessment, you can get an early indication of a person's potential before you make any calls on them at all," says PepsiCo International's Brian Chitester.

CSL Behring also assesses for learning agility, which the company equates with being "promotable." The company's Director of Organizational Development, Laurie Cowan, explains: "A willingness to develop is a key part of what we look for in putting people in the promotable category. The willingness to either move to another position or take on broader responsibilities as needed is a key factor."

Both managers and HR people are in a good position to assess job performance. Global specialty chemicals company Altana relies on members of its senior management team to identify high-potential employees. "We have grown from a number of family-owned businesses," explains Altana's Paul Mayer, "so members of the senior management team – the president and the general managers – frequently have been with the company for many years. These senior managers are therefore the ones who get to know the people with high potential based on their work performance and attitudes."

Wendy Watson is one senior executive who keeps her eye on job performance to identify MVPs for her company, State Street Corporation. But the Executive Vice President of Global Services doesn't rely just on her own observations: "To make sure that my views of top talent are confirmed, I usually reach out and talk to people who have been exposed to my top talent."

Talent Assessment Review Sessions

The assessments of managers and HR people are usually part of a more comprehensive approach to assessment. Most companies I interviewed incorporate their managers' assessments of job performance into talent assessment review sessions. Most review meetings take place annually, although there are exceptions: MDS, for example, holds them every six months.

For many companies, talent assessment reviews begin at the business unit level to identify people with high potential across the business units. These reviews are conducted at a meeting that usually involves the head of the business unit and its senior team, as well as representatives from HR. Assessments are made using data obtained through performance reviews and on-the-job experience. Employees are evaluated on such things as results they have achieved, their leadership competencies, and their adherence to company values.

From the review sessions, the names of high-potential employees are typically passed on to the CEO, who may then hold a talent review meeting with his or her senior business and function leaders to confirm their high-potential employees and potential successors.

Bob Hedley describes the talent review process at Maple Leaf Foods. "In our talent review sessions, we look at the individuals' values, their consistent performance, the results they have achieved versus the expectations we have for them, their career aspirations, and their potential in their current job, as well as their potential up to the next level or two in the company."

All salaried employees at Maple Leaf Foods are given this kind of review, what Hedley calls a "Leadership Edge Review." The reviews are held on five levels: executive council, management committee, senior managers, individual contributors, and analysts and administrators. "All five levels go through Leadership Edge Review," Hedley explains. "Our CEO sits in on 26 leadership review meetings and will see the performance assessment of the top 500 managers of the company."

During the review sessions, Maple Leaf Foods ranks its employees according to specifically defined categories. I'll be discussing ranking systems and grids in more detail below.

Raytheon Corporation's talent assessment process consists of a series of talent succession plan reviews, which culminate in a corporate-level annual strategic talent review meeting. At this corporate level, the review consists of a dialogue about the company's high-potential candidates, with the business presidents each presenting their lists to the CEO, who then opens the floor to discussion, so that other business presidents have the opportunity to describe the experiences they have had with the individual in question. "This really allows for an exchange of views," explains Raytheon's Senior Manager of Talent

Management and Succession Planning, Daniel Sonsino. "You're obviously going to have already championed a certain individual by putting them on the list, but the dialogue opens them up to additional feedback and input on how they performed in other business units."

The process at LoJack Corporation, similar to the one used at Raytheon, highlights the importance of consensus – as well as organization-wide support of the individual once consensus has been reached. Mark Bornemann describes this process, which is used after a person has been listed as "high-potential" using the 9-box grid (see description on page 33).

> I require the functional heads to talk for a couple of minutes on each candidate and give the reasons why they were identified as a high-potential. Then the operating committee is expected to challenge them from their own experience of that person. Then it's up to the functional head and the rest of the group to both validate the choice and give the thumbs up that they will support that individual throughout the organization. We don't want any silos built. If a person gets listed as a high-po, everyone on the operating committee has to sign off and agree that throughout that individual's career they will get support from the entire group, even if it's cross-functional.

Challenges in Identifying MVPs

Talent assessment review sessions are not foolproof: there is potential for either overestimation or underestimation of talent. Some managers may believe that all of their staff members are MVPs and refuse to differentiate between them. Other managers may want to hide their talent, as we saw in Chapter 2, fearing that if they identify their best performers, these individuals will be moved to other areas and their team's performance will suffer as a result. However, Sonsino warns against hiding your MVPs – particularly if your CEO, like Raytheon's, has been with the company for so long that he or she knows the employees well.

"You can't bury folks when you get in front of the CEO," says Sonsino. "The CEO knows so many people in the company, and he's going to call you on it if he doesn't believe a person you've put forward should be on the list, or if he thinks you're overlooking someone who's not on the list. If you've buried your best performer, you've just stuck your foot in your mouth in front of your boss, which is something people avoid like the plague around here."

Overestimating or underestimating talent is not always deliberate; reading talent can become much more "murky," as Sonsino puts it, when it comes to emerging talent. He explains Raytheon's solution: "We like to have our senior leaders sponsor or mentor our emerging talent so that the senior talent can get to know them and become familiar with their capabilities." And the benefits of such mentorship, says Sonsino, go both ways: "It gives the emerging talent the exposure to leadership as well."

Comparisons as a Means of Aiding Assessments

What Daniel Sonsino sees personally as the most valuable approach to assessment is the process of comparing MVPs with each other. "When you compare MVPs against the entire population, they do no wrong, but when you put them all in a bucket, as it were, and compare them against each other, then you start to see different tiers in their capabilities and you can select out your top talent. If you can then map those capabilities against your company's idea of the leader of the future, you've got another gage. Those are really the two gages, the comparison with other MVPs and the comparison against the future executive."

Assessment Tools and Methods Championed by Companies

Most companies I interviewed do not rely solely on the opinions of senior managers or executives – even if those opinions are informed and seconded by other executives. Most talent assessment processes also rely on assessment tools and ranking grids that measure potential methodically and objectively. There are a vast array of assessment tools, both on the market and created by companies themselves – far too many to describe in this chapter. Below I've highlighted a few key tools in the context of how companies are putting them to use and to what effect. A more detailed description of the tools and assessment approaches described in this chapter, and many more besides, can be found in Appendix 2.

9-Box Grid

One tool that companies find particularly useful in helping them to identify their talent is the 9-box grid. A 9-box grid plots potential (low, medium, high) against performance (low, medium, high) to create a grid of nine categories of people, ranging from low potential/low performance to high potential/high performance. Below is an example of a 9-box grid, followed by definitions of the people that fit in each category, that I have used for talent assessment in a number of organizations.

Talent Management Assessment: 9 – Box Grid

<table>
<tr><td rowspan="2"></td><td></td><td colspan="3">PERFORMANCE</td></tr>
<tr><td></td><td>Low</td><td>Medium</td><td>High</td></tr>
<tr><td rowspan="6">POTENTIAL</td><td rowspan="2">High</td><td>Hi Po/Lo Per
6</td><td>Hi Po/Med Per
8</td><td>Hi Po/Hi Per
9</td></tr>
<tr><td>Diamond in the Rough</td><td>Future High Potential</td><td>High Potential</td></tr>
<tr><td rowspan="2">Medium</td><td>Med Po/Lo Per
3</td><td>Med Po/Med Per
5</td><td>Med Po/Hi Per
7</td></tr>
<tr><td>Inconsistent Performer Potential</td><td>Key Performer</td><td>Adaptable Professional with Potential</td></tr>
<tr><td rowspan="2">Low</td><td>Lo Po/Lo Per
1</td><td>Lo Po/Med Per
2</td><td>Lo Po/Hi Per
4</td></tr>
<tr><td>Low Performer Future Analysis</td><td>Future High Professional Stabilizer</td><td>High Professional</td></tr>
</table>

Continued

Talent Management Assessment: 9 – Box Grid—*continued*

6	8	9
• In general limited experience in role • Does not fulfill current duties to optimum level • Has potential to improve	• Exceeds on requirements and expectations of the job/role and/or • Exceeds on personal performance goals • Has high degree of flexibility beyond current role • Has general manager ability	• Exceeds on requirements and expectations of the job/role and/or • Exceeds on personal performance goals • Shapes culture and strategy • Can handle much greater responsibility
3	**5**	**7**
• Limited experience in role • Does not meet required expectations • Has potential to assume greater responsibility in the future	• Meets all requirements and expectations of the job/role and/or • Achieves all personal performance goals • Orientation to growth and results in keeping with current position • Well developed managerial skills	• Good execution of current tasks • Potential for increased responsibility or another position • Highly flexible
1	**2**	**4**
• Does not fully achieve all personal performance goals • Needs coaching to see if another position is more suitable • Does not meet requirements and expectations of the job/role	• High degree of professional know-how • Needs clearly defined goals • May be limited in motivation and managerial power • Niche player with limited mobility	• Performance exceeds expectation • Needs clearly defined goals • Maybe limited in motivation • Niche player with poor prospects for mobility

It is individuals whose attributes correspond to the top right box that companies are keen to retain and develop. As LoJack's Mark Bornemann puts it: "These are the people who really drive the leadership development, the super top talent. Consider them the movers and shakers, and do what you can to retain them."

Current Estimated Potential

Current Estimated Potential (CEP) is a concept that has been developed by, and belongs to, Shell International – a company well recognized for its ability to assess potential. Shell's Vice President of Resourcing and Development, Mike Conway, explains that CEP is used at Shell to assess or more realistically estimate the potential of its employees. It is based on three key criteria: Capacity, Achievement, and Relationships. Based on these criteria, CEP estimates whether a person has the potential to progress to senior management and executive management levels. Every professional and management staff member at Shell is measured for his or her potential against these criteria. Conway points out that although the tool has been used in the company for some years, "each part of the Company has done the exercise to different timetables and somewhat different standards of execution. So 2008 is the first year that we will really have a single, consistent group-wide execution of a CEP exercise. This means a single set of messages to staff and managers, a common timetable and consistent standards of coaching and training for those leading the process."

Corporate Leadership Council Identification Tool

Two of the organizations I interviewed use the Corporate Leadership Council (CLC) approach/criteria – as touched on in Chapter 2. The characteristics of potential considered in this leading-edge assessment tool are Aspiration, Engagement, and Ability. One of the companies is enthusiastic about the way the CLC tool has helped the company "drill down to a better understanding of potential."

> We use the CLC's three characteristics, aspiration, engagement and ability, as the lenses for looking at potential and determining who is truly a high-potential here. The tool really helps us to determine who has learning agility – the openness to learning more about themselves and about the business.
>
> This tool is really helpful because it frames potential in such a way that people can begin to understand what potential really is. For instance, it says that even though I like Jane and she's fabulous in what she does, if I use this model and she shouldn't rate highly in all three dimensions, she can't be considered

high-potential. For instance, if you don't aspire to greater things, you will not advance and be engaged. If you're not engaged with the organization, you're not going to be there. And if you lack agility, either in terms of learning or openness to doing things differently, you're not going to get there.

Naomi Shaw is equally enthusiastic about the CLC tool, which her company, Scotiabank, uses as a component of its talent review sessions. "It's absolutely great," says Shaw. "We've merged our emphasis on experiences, values and performance with the CLC criteria of aspiration, engagement and ability, and it helps us ensure consistency in how we identify our key people, our high-pos. We then calibrate it at our round-table discussions."

Other Ranking Categories and Grids

Several other companies have also created categories and grids against which they rank their employees. At the conclusion of each talent review session, Maple Leaf Foods ranks its employees according to one of four categories, as described by Bob Hedley:

1. Business excellence – "A highly values consistent role model, consistent in their leadership and performance driven. They attain results on a consistent basis and their results exceed expectations."
2. Business driver – "An employee who is very values consistent, achieves slightly less than in the business excellence category in values and/or results versus expectations."
3. Key contributor – "A solid professional who goes about their work and gets the job done."
4. High intervention – "Someone who needs help to develop further or needs to be moved elsewhere where they may be more successful in the company or managed out."

Hedley stresses that *all* employees are valued, no matter where they fall in the forced ranking, but adds that the ranking does govern how the company will invest in their development and future. "Certainly somebody who's considered a business excellence performer is going to have an enriched developmental action plan."

Hogan Assessment Tools

Many companies, including PepsiCo, mentioned the Hogan suite of assessment tools, developed by Hogan Assessment Systems. Steve Doerflein of the organizational consulting firm Right Management provided me with a brief description of each component of the suite and why this assessment tool is now more widely used:

- Hogan Personality Inventory (HPI) – "Gives an idea of how an individual faces the world and operates on a day-to-day basis."
- Hogan Development Survey (HDS) – "Provides an idea of the dark side of a person's personality and their potential derailers – interpersonal characteristics that can cause people to have problems in a stressful situation."
- Motives, Values, Preferences Inventory (MVPI) – "Provides information that helps you understand how a person might fit into a new culture or change the existing culture."

Leadership Futures President Karen Steadman points out that MVPs themselves like the Hogan suite of assessment tools. "It gives them a full picture of what they are doing well and what their potential derailers are. I think MVPs love that information." For more details on the Hogan suite of assessment tools, see Appendix 2.[1]

Bring in the Experts

Some companies bring in external experts to do the testing and assessment of their high-potentials or to confirm their own internal testing. This is the case for both Rogers Communications and MDS Inc.

MDS Inc. brings in an organizational psychologist to help with its management assessments, because, as Jim Reid explains, "you're really benchmarking talent against what you might call an executive norm group." The psychologist helps the company gage its high-potential employees by helping it to "get a sense of what their cognitive ability is, what their integrative skills are, what their orientation is around people and relationships and teams."

---

1 A recent book that readers interested in the Hogan Development Survey may find useful is *Why CEOs Fail: The Eleven Behaviors that Can Derail Your Climb to the Top – and How to Manage Them*, by David L. Dotlich and Peter C. Cairo, Jossey-Bass, 2003.

Rogers Communications brings in external consultants to do assessments every couple of years. "We'll bring in a search firm with psychometric testing," explains Senior Vice President and Chief Human Resource Officer, Kevin Pennington. "They'll do behavioral event interviews and a series of tests."

Pennington also makes another novel use of external "experts" for assessment purposes: keeping tabs on how the labor market values Rogers' employees. "It's nice to know that we have what we think is an MVP," he explains, "but are they considered an MVP in the market? I like to know all the search people who could be contacting our MVPs and what they think about them. So we do a market assessment of our talent, as well as a performance assessment."

The Role of Assessment and Development Centers

Companies definitely play a key role in making internal assessments of their most valuable performers, or in bringing in outside consultants to assist. Increasingly, however, companies are also identifying or confirming their high-potential employees through the use of independent assessment and development centers. An assessment center is not always an actual place, but rather a process of looking at individuals using multiple measures and exercises, and multiple assessors. An assessment center provides an objective way for companies to identify and/or validate their high-potential employees. As Steve Doerflein points out, "Many companies identify the people internally that they think are the ones who should be the lifeblood of the organization and have the capacity to take the next step up. These companies have used the measurements from their assessment activities to get a fuller, richer look at the individual. What they typically want from an assessment center is something more structured that can provide a more objective look at the individual."

Joy McGovern, who is Practice Leader of the assessment practice at Right Management in the northeastern U.S., and her colleague Steve Doerflein provided me with details on the key components of assessment centers. They began by outlining the multiple purposes served by assessment centers:

- Ensuring that the right people are in the right positions
- Identifying the people who are most likely to be successful in the organization

- Developing a talent pool for effective succession planning
- Targeting developmental activities for the highest return on investment

The fundamental method used by an assessment center is the observation of people's behaviors by multiple assessors as they are put through simulations or "exercises" that resemble situations and problems relevant to the job and level under consideration. The following are typical tools for performance observation and evaluation used in most centers:

- Feedback on the individual's 360-degree assessments. These assessments consist of questions on a number of leadership competencies that are either specific to the company or generic to leadership positions. The 360s are usually completed by the person's manager, a sample of their peers, and a sample of their staff. (See the latter part of this chapter and Appendix 2 for more details on 360-degree assessments.)
- Feedback on a battery of assessment tools such as Hogan, Choices Learning Agility, and FIRO-B. (Again, for details on these and other tools, see Appendix 2.)
- Simulation exercises to allow the individual to try on what it would be like to be in a higher level role.
- Role plays with staff members.
- Role plays with managers.
- Role plays with peers.
- Role plays of customer situations.
- Behavioral interviews to ask the individual what they did in specific situations.
- A simulated presentation made by the individual to their manager or board, based on complex information, to determine how well they think on their feet.
- Leaderless group discussions, in which each person has an equal position, to determine who collaborates and who doesn't, who asks the right questions, and who takes on the leadership role.
- The use of in-basket exercises to assess the individual's prioritization skills and ability to determine when to involve others in the decision-making process.

Doerflein stresses the particular value assessment centers have in simulating high-level positions and situations. "The further up in the organization you go, the more you have to connect with people. In our peer role play, we sometimes see people who just aren't used to considering the views of others. They're so focused on what they need to accomplish and may be so results-oriented that they fail to see where their peers are coming from." By putting someone in a simulated situation, interpersonal characteristics like these, which might not be obvious in their current job, may show up.

Michael Lindemann, who has experience with working with a number of well known global companies explains, before going to the assessment center, the selected employees attended a leadership workshop, "where they were exposed to the latest thinking on leadership, and they had very senior company executives coming in as guest speakers."

Lindemann goes on to explain what happened for the employees at the assessment center.

> Each person was assigned their own individual executive coach. They then went through a 360-degree survey process, and their coach interviewed their boss and a couple of peers, as well as a couple of direct reports. They also completed a variety of leadership profiles, including Hogan. They then went through a full day of very carefully customized business simulations, which faithfully reproduced their working environment, and they were observed in various situations. Their executive coach then gave them integrated feedback. The employees had access to the coach for a specified number of additional hours to complete the program, and they could also pay an additional fee and extend the coaching if they chose to do so.

The assessments provided by these centers can also become the foundation for putting together development plans for your MVPs, which we will discuss further in the next section.

Assessment for Creating Development Plans

Assessments are used not only to determine or confirm who your MVPs are, but also to create effective development plans for them. These plans help high-potential employees to learn and grow and to be ready to take on larger or broader roles within the organization. The creation of development plans often relies heavily on the use of assessment tools – to help management determine the appropriate direction for each individual.

Procter & Gamble has a philosophy that every employee has a work development plan. P&G's Director of Human Resources, Keith Lawrence, explains how it works:

> The work development plan includes a number of things, including annual results from the previous year against whatever work plan they had identified, together with their priorities and goals. It also includes a statement of the feedback and a specific development plan that includes how you can better leverage your strengths in the year ahead.

As part of this plan, individuals have a one-page assessment of their leadership capabilities, based on the P&G definition of leadership. "So if we find an individual is struggling in the area of leadership, we'll obtain some additional feedback from the organization about their leadership to give them some additional insight into what they might be able to do to become a better leader," explains Lawrence.

Individualized Custom Programming

A number of companies I interviewed mentioned that once their employees have been identified as MVPs or high-potentials, they attend programs that have been specifically designed for them. These programs usually include some form of assessment that helps the individuals create development plans that build on their strengths and help remove any potential derailers. PepsiCo International and Shell International are two companies that invest in such programming.

For its people who have the potential ultimately to reach the most senior positions in the company, Shell invests in an executive leadership program that has two components. The "Assessment for Development" stage uses Shell senior managers and external faculty working together to identify competence gaps, explains Shell's Mike Conway. The second stage is then a learning program that aims to put the emerging leaders on a path to both grow their understanding of the role and demands of senior leadership and address their own specific development needs.

Brian Chitester describes the program for high-potentials at PepsiCo. "As part of the program, we bring in Dr. Marty Seldman.

Prior to attending the session, the participants take his assessments on SOCIAL STYLES(sm) and organization savvy. He then comes in and runs workshops on SOCIAL STYLES and savvy and gives the participants the results of their assessment to bolster self-awareness."

The Role of Assessment Centers in Development Plans

As mentioned above, assessment centers can play an important role in creating development plans for MVPs. As Steve Doerflein explains, "We are not talking just about what sort of workshop they should be engaged in; we are really talking about strategies for someone to work at. There are many times when they will be shying away from taking on a certain task or doing something they really should be making a contribution to."

The Role of Assessment Tools in Creating Development Plans

Some companies use the following tools as part of their high potential leadership development programs.

- 360-degree process
- MBTI Step II
- California Personality Inventory
- Conflict Dynamics 360
- BarOn Emotional Quotient Scale

They also use individual coaches, who work with the MVP throughout the year to bolster the feedback the individual receives from these assessment instruments. As we will see below, assessments play a major role in the coaching process.

Assessment as Part of the Coaching Process

Many individual development plans include the use of coaching. Sometimes coaching is part of an integrated leadership development plan, as we will see in Chapter 4; sometimes it is a stand-alone development process. In either case, a robust coaching engagement depends on clearly identifying behavioral changes that are required and areas of development that need addressing. In the case of coaching that is part of an integrated leadership development plan, the coach often uses the results of the assessments that were used to create the plan. However, if the coaching is a stand-alone process, it will be necessary for the coach and/or organization to collect information on the individual's competencies and areas in need of development. Collecting this information, through assessments, will enable the coach, coachee, their manager, and HR to determine the key priorities that need to be addressed during the coaching process.

Some of the coaches and coaching leaders from Right Management that I spoke with were Winnie Lanoix, Ed Piccolino, Paul Larson, and Arabelle Fedora. They outlined the typical types of assessments they use as part of the coaching process:

- Myers-Briggs Step II
- FIRO-B and Leadership Report
- LSI
- Hogan Suite

Many of the other tools used to do these assessments are the same as those that have been described in previous sections of this chapter.

Use of 360-Degree Interviews

One assessment tool particularly favored by coaches is 360-degree interviewing. In Chapter 2, I noted the widespread use companies make of 360-degree assessment tools and surveys. However, when it comes to coaching, many coaches find that these tools are not always useful in identifying areas for development of the already highly regarded individual. The reason for this is that more often than not MVPs are rated as 5s on all of the competency scales, where 1 is low and 5 is very high. When the person is already perceived to be at the top of their game, there is very little room left to determine areas in need of improvement.

Arabelle Fedora told me a story that highlights the challenge of using the 360-degree survey.

> One of our coaches called me after reviewing a 360 survey report in which an MVP he is coaching had been rated all 5s. The coach and I had to look really hard to find anything in the 360 that

begged additional investigation – it was like looking for a needle in a haystack. Ultimately we found a few rater inconsistencies to be explored.

It is these kinds of challenges in obtaining helpful information from 360-degree surveys that spur coaches on to perform 360 interviews. Coach Ed Piccolino, who is also President of Piccolino Associates, LLC, elaborates on the advantages of the face-to-face interview. "Personally I don't find the established psychometric tools around the 360 process all that helpful, especially with MVPs. I find that you need to go through a much more penetrating face-to-face series of interviews to get really granular at a truly behavioral level about it. Otherwise, you get this positive halo and no learning from it." As Piccolino points out, strengths always have a dark side, and with MVPs, it is important to get the deeper, more complete picture. This picture is what will emerge from 360 interviews, which, like the surveys, are conducted with the coachees, their managers, a sample of their staff, and a sample of their peers. They may also include interviews with other key stakeholders. Piccolino adds, "…there is tremendous power in triangulating the findings from all of these interviews, and then combining those inputs with the other professional assessment tools looking for consistent patterns or themes in the data."

Leadership Futures President Karen Steadman uses the interviews to challenge her coachees, who are already successful, to leap to greater heights. "When I interview people I'm saying, 'You've been successful, how do we relaunch your brand, how do we enhance your brand, how do we make sure it's stronger, how do we go out and assess how your brand is being perceived by your stakeholders?' This is why we need to do 360 interviews."

Typical Questions Asked in 360 Interviews

Right Management's Senior Vice President of Career Management Consulting, Dina Lichtman, outlines the typical questions she asks when conducting a 360 interview.

- What does this person do well?
- What do you think would be the impact to the organization without them?

- How do they communicate?
- What would their peers say about this individual?
- What would their manager and their subordinates say about them?
- How will you know if there has been a change in behaviors or competencies?
- Is this an organization that will accept a new behavior?
- Is this an organization that says it wants change but ultimately when they see it they may not want it?
- How does this organization sabotage change in others?
- What does success look like to you? How will you know it when you see it?
- If there was one magic statement you could make that would make this person more successful, what would that be?

MVPs' Response to Assessment

So you've put your MVPs and your high-potential employees through a battery of assessment tools and processes, and you've determined who your high-potentials are and embarked on a development plan for them. But what is the effect of all this testing on the individuals themselves? Many might find all these tests and exercises daunting. But – significantly enough – not the MVPs. Says Karen Steadman: "MVPs like to measure themselves and set goals and targets, so I think they actually like assessments, more than others perhaps do."

PepsiCo International's Brian Chitester agrees. He cites well-known industrial and organizational psychologist Dr. Robert Eichinger's theory that high-potential people are more self-aware than others and are hungry to have feedback and to know about themselves.

State Street's Wendy Watson also understands this characteristic of MVPs – she capitalizes on it. "When I get positive feedback about the people I consider my top talent, I encourage those individuals to seek that feedback directly."

So if you find yourself with an employee who thrives on participating in the assessment process and is eager for feedback, that in itself may be an indicator that you have someone of high potential in your company – yet another benefit of applying a rigorous assessment approach throughout your organization.

Summary of Assessment Approaches and Tools

- Assessments are used to identify MVPs, develop a work plan for MVPs, and assist in the coaching of MVPs.

- Key approaches to assessment include:

  - evaluation of job performance
  - holding of talent review sessions
  - use of commercial and custom-designed measurement tools and ranking grids
  - bringing in the experts
  - identifying or confirming high-potential employees through the use of assessment centers.

- MVPs respond positively to assessments and are hungry for feedback to learn more about themselves.

CHAPTER 4

Approaches to Leadership Development

Once you've identified your MVPs and your high-potential staff, the greater challenge begins. How are you going to develop them? How are you going to ensure that they continue to perform at consistently high levels and, more important, that they remain challenged and capable of taking on broader roles within the organization? This chapter looks at approaches to development taken by major, successful organizations and considers the contributions of coaching.

In the past, companies often regarded coaching as a way to "fix" people when they had performance issues. Coaching was often used as a last-ditch effort to improve a person's performance and if this did not happen, then the individual was "out the door." Small wonder then that people resisted having a coach!

High-potential people may still perceive coaching as a way to overcome potential derailers. This coaching is certainly not a "fix-it" type of coaching for performance issues. For example, Teri Kozikowski at GE Real Estate explains that the company turns to coaches when "a person has great potential and can achieve great results, but has some behaviors or skill deficiencies that can derail them. I've seen great analytic talent take it to the nth degree losing themselves in the detail and ultimately losing sight of the deliverable at hand. I've also seen people who are so amiable, they may be incorrectly perceived as not great at delivering results. For instance, I've worked with a particular leader in the Sales organization. The problem is that he is so good at the relationship piece – so charismatic – that people remember the fun guy and don't see the high-quality technical salesperson underneath who achieves great results. So, in areas like this, we would employ a coach. The coaching intervention is very targeted."

Increasingly, however, organizations are defining a new and arguably more effective role for coaching. They are realizing that it is far better to spend coaching dollars on MVPs and high-potential people within the context of a broad and integrated approach to development. "I will tell you," observes coach Ed Piccolino of Piccolino Associates, LLC, "that, when [coaching] is integrated, it's far more impactful, and it helps the company establish its brand as a talent development 'factory' and a place with real talent 'muscle,' which I'm convinced has more impact on stock price, as a lever, than any other HR initiative I can think of. It makes it so much easier to build the bench. It takes years to build that differentiator brand; so it really is a wonderful competitive advantage."

In many ways PepsiCo International has set the standard for developing high-potential, high-performance employees using a comprehensive and integrated approach. Based on the work of Dr. Robert Eichinger and the HR team, PepsiCo's widely discussed 70-20-10 model declares that 70 percent of development takes place through on-the-job experience, 20 percent through coaching, and 10 percent through formal learning. MVP development at PepsiCo is built around this fundamental insight.

As described by PepsiCo's Brian Chitester, the process begins with the identification of MVPs. The company has a career growth model available to all employees. It involves a performance management system that sets objectives, gives feedback, and provides performance ratings. Employees who perform well within this system are subjected to four additional assessments, as described by Chitester:

> One is determination of leadership capabilities, which comes out of assessment against our leadership 360 process.
>
> The next one addresses functional excellence. We have functional competency models for most of our functions and job profiles for most multi-incumbent jobs.
>
> Another tests for knowledge of the business. It is knowing more than just what you're working on. If you're a marketing guy it means understanding sales and operations; for a beverage guy it means understanding snacks and foods as well. We have training for this.

The fourth piece is critical experiences. We've identified 15 critical experiences that make up a senior leader at PepsiCo. These include start-ups, global assignments, job rotations, etcetera.

Once past these hurdles, the MVP candidate is considered eligible for assuming new leadership roles and for enrollment in the company's talent management program based on the 70-20-10 development model taught by Dr. Eichinger.

The next step in the process involves the narrowest, 10 percent segment of this model, formal training. Potential MVPs attend the International Leadership Development Program (ILDP), a six-day program led by the company's CEO. "What's more powerful," asks Chitester, "than spending six days with the CEO, who sits in the room the whole time, who teaches several of the modules – including strategy, including change management, including values – who never leaves the room, doesn't get on his Blackberry, doesn't make or take phone calls, doesn't set up other meetings, and who engages in every conversation that occurs? It's a way to see inside the senior-most executive's head. Everybody has breakfast with him, everybody has dinner with him. It becomes a critical experience for a group of people who typically don't have a line of sight to him. So it's extremely powerful. We take a different class of 32 there every year based on future-leader calls."

Coaching, the 20 percent segment, follows formal training: "You need a coach who can help integrate all that information from the ILDP, because after spending six days with us your brain is pretty full," explains Chitester. "You need somebody to help you sort through this material and that's when the coach comes in." From this point on, the coaches at PepsiCo International do the bulk of their work. Even before potential MVPs attend the ILDP, in fact, coaches sit in on feedback sessions between the MVPs and their Hogan consultants (for more on Hogan assessment tools, see Chapter 3 and Appendix 2). Says Chitester: "The coach picks up the development plan and works with the [MVP] for six to nine months. Then we track that interaction through a Web site where, on three occasions, the coach posts what he or she is working on with the person." MVPs are encouraged to think about their experiences on the job and to consider how they might augment the work of their managers, who also serve as the MVPs' internal coaches. It is worth noting that the coaching function at PepsiCo International involves both internal and external coaching. We will take a closer look at internal and external coaches in Chapter 5.

The final element in the PepsiCo development process, the 70 percent segment, focuses on development through carefully planned job experience. Providing people with experience in a variety of different jobs is a major part of the process. As Chitester explains, "After about 28 to 36 months, we look at how long high-potentials or MVPs have been there. Have they got from that experience what they were supposed to? If it's time to move them, where are they going? What experiences are we trying to expose them to in their next role? Then we actually try to move people."

PepsiCo's 70-20-10 model represents a particularly sophisticated example of an integrated and comprehensive approach to MVP development. It includes four of the five elements most commonly found in the development models used by the firms interviewed for this book:

- Assessment and development plan creation
- Formal training
- Individual development
- On-the-job development

In the remainder of this chapter, I will examine each of these elements and the role of coaching in greater detail. A fifth element, action team learning projects, will also be examined. These might profitably be understood as a special form of on-the-job development. Here, too, coaching plays a significant role.

Assessment and Development Plan Creation

Integrated MVP development programs invariably begin with formal assessments and the creation of a far-reaching development plan. While I have already dealt with assessment tools and approaches to identifying talent in Chapter 3, I would like to return to the subject here with specific reference to the role of assessment in integrated development programs. Within the context of such programs, coaches play a significant role in delivering assessment feedback and helping shape development plans. These plans are usually reviewed and confirmed by managers, and sometimes also by HR departments.

When they are part of a more extensive integrated development program, assessments and the creation of development plans often involve an elaborate process touching on other elements of the integrated program. The coach's contribution, however, goes beyond helping with the plan itself. He or she will also meet with the MVP's managers "to determine the challenges and the skills and strengths MVPs have to build in order to be successful in the role for which they are a designated successor. So the focus is really on the next level of position or role for the individual." The coach's responsibilities also include the traditional function of helping MVPs identify some of the "derailers that are going to throw them off track if they don't deal with them before they get to the next level."

In many organizations, assessment and assessment coaching are closely connected with the formal training component of the integrated program. At UBS Investment Bank, group-based coach-assisted assessment debriefing takes place during a three-day off-site training session called the Leader View. As Michelle Blieberg, Managing Director and Global Learning Officer at UBS Investment Bank explains, "At the Leader View, MVPs get feedback from a variety of assessment tools. We then divide the groups into quads and each quad gets a professional external coach. The coach's role is to encourage these people to tell their story – to share the good things they've learned about themselves, the surprises, the revelations and what they think they need to work on. This is the group that's always gotten As in school. This is the group that gets the top rating on their performance reviews. So, often, they've never got this information and feedback about themselves, which is so important."

At Royal Dutch Shell, assessment and initial debriefing occurs during a residential program. Says Shell's Mike Conway: "We have short residential programs where participants go through extensive assessment and end up with a development plan. This event provides some fairly in-depth analysis of the individual's performance over a couple of days of observed behavior and the assessment is firmly against nine leadership competency areas or, in Shell language 'The Nine Planets'. We identify areas of strength, areas where there's further development required, and those areas where there is significant weakness." The process, including the preparation and follow up, provides an atmosphere conducive to intensive self-reflection: "Probably most of what we get out of this process is the insight the participants gain around the significant challenges and expectations when stepping up to senior leadership," says Conway. "This shows up in many ways but for example this assessment is often the first time they really have to examine their ability to deliver results through other people rather than through their own professional skills or hard work."

HR staff and a faculty member, generally a senior line manager, provide follow up to the event. "The individual gets their full report and are required to set up a meeting with their HR Advisor, their line manager, and the faculty member who was part of the assessment team," explains Conway. "Through this meeting, the faculty member passes responsibility back into the organization. The individual will use this process to articulate their own individual development plan and get support and guidance to pursue the agreed path. This ensures alignment between the manager and the employee around development.

As Conway explains, the resulting development plans tend to focus on behavioral change. "It's about addressing those aspects of leadership behavior that often can be worked on in real time in the current role. Individuals may need some guidance and coaching from their line manager, they may need help from HR, or they may need specific training." Development plans also try to identify how the individual can develop through future job experience: "For example, someone who's been ten years working in a technical discipline may really need to take a role that enhances their capability in terms of commercial exposure. Training can help, but at Shell it is often done through the next job assignment. Sometimes a development need can opportunistically be met by a short-term project assignment."

At CSL Behring, assessment and development coaching serve as bookends to formal training. Laurie Cowan, Director of Organizational Development, explains that before participating in a residential Global Leadership Program, MVPs receive a 360-degree assessment and "get some coaching in order to debrief the feedback received in the 360." After the residential training program has been completed, the coach and MVP reconvene to draw up a development plan.

Clearly, the assessment-training-planning sequence indicates that prior assessment influences what occurs during formal training and that formal training, in turn, is essential to the creation of the development plan. As in most of the examples I have been discussing, formal training involving coaching plays an important role in assessment and in creating the development plan.

Formal Training

Almost all integrated development programs for MVPs involve formal training that goes well beyond assessment and development planning. It can involve instruction in such topics as company values, strategy, client needs, leadership, technical skills, and functional skills, to name just a few. While coaching by actual coaches is typically confined to assessment and development, coaching and mentoring are often informally provided by training leaders, usually senior managers or even the company CEO. At Canada's Scotiabank, coaching itself is a subject on the organization's formal training agenda. Says Naomi Shaw, Scotiabank's Vice President of Leadership: "We have an in-house coaching program for vice presidents and above, which involves e-learning and a workshop that focuses on building their coaching skills."

Similarly, at Procter & Gamble, training is done on-site by company leaders supported by HR. They organize sessions where, as Keith Lawrence explains, "Some best-in-class external resources come in for specific topics. For example, P&G is expanding broadly into the beauty business, so we tapped into the CEO of a well-known retail store who started at Procter & Gamble many years ago, who came to the session and talked about the industry and what's necessary to stay in touch with emerging times. We have had individuals like John Chambers come from Cisco to talk about the role of technology in the marketplace and how that can transform P&G's business. We've also brought in senior leaders from retailers such as Wal-Mart and Target to talk about not only what their business is like but how P&G is meeting their needs. On a very frequent basis, we expose employees at all levels to our consumers so they are really in touch with the external marketplace."

As we have seen, many organizations send their MVPs and high-potential employees off site for intensive residential training sessions. Over a two-year period, UBS Investment Bank, for example, sends its potential leaders on three three-day residential off-site sessions known as the Leader View, the Team View, and the Client View. Two of the off-site sessions involve intensive coaching. GE Real Estate goes so far as to send nominated high performers on multi-week experiential learning courses held at its dedicated training facility, the John F. Welch Center, also known as Crotonville. Not the least of the benefits afforded by such residencies is the opportunity for networking they provide. As GE's Teri Kozikowski explains, Crotonville "allows you to network with people who are going to be your peers as you continue to grow in the organization. You're building a network, you're getting exposed to leadership, and you're getting exposed to GE strategy."

Other organizations send their promising people to established academic institutions. Keith Lawrence of Procter & Gamble estimates that about 5 percent of the company's senior managers are sent to programs at Harvard Business School or to the Looking Glass program at the Center for Creative Leadership. MDS Nordion, like Procter & Gamble, makes use of the programs offered by the Center for Creative Leadership. But the company will also send its most promising leaders to do MBAs.

Uniquely, some organizations combine their own internal resources with the resources offered by external learning institutions. Maple Leaf Foods, for example, runs a company "Leadership Academy" in partnership with the Ivey School of Business at the University of Western Ontario in London, Ontario. Development is provided by both the school's faculty and the company's senior managers. While "Ivey faculty play a role in designing the program and delivering certain key case studies and the like," explains Maple Leaf's Bob Hedley, "our own Maple Leaf leaders carry over 50 percent of the time on the floor with the employees."

Organizations whose training programs fall on the more elaborate end of the scale tend to customize their programs to meet the needs of MVPs at different stages of their careers. Maple Leaf, for example, offers leadership programs at four levels. Training, as well as coaching and mentoring, is provided by the CEO and core executive council members. As described by Bob Hedley, the first level consists of a foundation program sponsored by the company's CEO: "In the Foundations program we do a deep dive on feedback and values. We introduce them to the other strategic principles of the company, the state of the business, and we start to look at leadership in terms of decisiveness, action, and results." The subsequent programs, Hedley continues, are entitled Direct Personal Leadership I, II, and III. "The first one is about self-awareness and leading others and the beginnings of change management. The second one is designed around challenging conversations specific to Maple Leaf and developing your conversational abilities. The third one is about implementing strategy and it's more of a senior program. The idea is that, as you progress in your career at Maple Leaf, you would return to the academy every two to three years and you would take another one of these leadership courses."

The executive training curriculum at GE consists of three levels: Manager Development Course (MDC), Business Management Course (BMC), and Executive Development Course (EDC). As Teri Kozikowski explains, "The first-level program introduces you in depth to GE strategy and strategists and how to incorporate those actions and directions into your role. The second-level course, BMC, is a much more experiential course, where the group does a consulting project. In the highest-level class, EDC, participants also do a lot of research, but they typically work on a concept rather than a defined project. The BMC and EDC programs allow our higher-level employees to do something that's pertinent to the business today." The GE program, like that at Maple Leaf Foods, ensures that learning for MVPs remains a long-term enterprise and that MVPs remain challenged as their careers progress.

Action Team Learning Projects

GE Real Estate's second- and third-level programs closely resemble action team learning projects, which are increasingly forming part of leadership development programs for high-potentials and MVPs. As the name suggests, MVPs work together in teams on a set project that can last as long as several months. The purpose is twofold: to set some of the organization's most talented people to work on tasks of real importance for the company, and to provide MVPs with experiences that will contribute to their professional growth. Teams are typically sponsored by the senior executive. They are also very often assigned coaches, who serve as a resource, provide direction on team effectiveness, offer business input, and counsel individual team members.

Scotiabank brings together approximately three teams at a time, each comprised of three to four high potentials from across the organization. These projects run for between four and eight months. The program at UBS Financial Services runs for three months. "Each year," Global Learning Officer Michelle Blieberg explains, "UBS runs approximately 26 action learning projects that these people work on."

Normally, MVPs work on these projects in addition to meeting their day-to-day responsibilities. Scotiabank, however, stands out as an exception to the norm. Here, MVPs are assigned to their action teams on a full-time basis. In other words, at Scotiabank MVPs are removed from their regular roles for a period of up to eight months. This practice indicates the value Scotiabank places on the action team experience. In Naomi Shaw's words, "We put most of our emphasis on experience-based learning."

Learning, however, is not the only explanation. The projects undertaken by Scotiabank's action teams have genuine significance for the business, usually involving "strategic thinking and strategic influencing." "Each one of these teams," says Shaw, "supports an executive working group who is working on a strategy business issue. Their recommendation on the strategic business issue is ultimately presented to Scotiabank's Board of Directors. This is a real-life action plan that requires some thinking."

Even those organizations whose team members are assigned team duties in addition to their regular responsibilities stress the real value of the projects. Chubb Insurance uses strategic action teams to get some high-profile initiatives underway. As Ellen Moore, President of Chubb Insurance Company, notes: "Some of our corporate initiatives are aligned with our business goals, and through a special nomination process, we put our best people on these teams. A great example involves a scenario planning project. The project is completely embedded in the business, and the people on the team are fascinated with the business aspect. It's a super experience for them and it's very challenging work." At UBS Financial Services, 60 percent of the outcomes of action learning projects have been implemented to some degree, which Barbara Cona Amone, Head of HR, Americas and Head of Global Talent, UBS Investment Bank, Managing Director and member of UBS Investment Bank Board notes, "has a phenomenal developmental value for them and real commercial value for the firm."

Not surprisingly, given the importance of many of the projects undertaken, action learning teams typically receive extensive support from top-level management. "Our President and CEO usually assigns one or two executives from his executive team to sponsor the team," Scotiabank's Naomi Shaw reports." UBS Financial Services actually trains senior managers on how to support action teams effectively. Barbara Cona Amone notes: "We have trained our senior-level sponsors in such things as how to align a team right away, what decision-making process to give them, how to outline for a team what your expectations are and what they need to deliver."

Coaching, finally, provides another essential layer of action team support. At Scotiabank, one-to-one coaching is provided internally by one of the bank's executives. Chubb uses internal learning coaches assigned to each project team. UBS Financial Services relies on both internal and external coaches. External coaches, says UBS Global Learning Officer Michelle Blieberg, "work on team dynamics and they also help the team accomplish their charter. They coach the quality of the research and they coach how well the presentation is structured and how it's presented."

Individual Development

While coaching can play an important role in all areas of integrated MVP development programs, it is typically used most intensively to support individual MVP development. In fact, as organizations are increasingly realizing, one-on-one coaching can be more effective in developing an MVP than formal training. Coaching is better able to focus on the MVP's specific needs and to concentrate on long-term success. It is often used, as Laurie Cowan of CSL Behring puts it, in a "very targeted" way to help prepare the MVP to meet particular company needs.

Many organizations, such as CSL Behring, turn to coaching to prepare MVPs for a move to a more senior leadership role. "We use coaching," says Cowan, "for specific pipeline growth and succession. This is very much focused on developing MVPs towards more senior levels of responsibility and leadership." Denise Lockaby of The Stride Rite Corporation says, "Coaching fits in most nicely when I have MVPs who are facing a new leadership challenge. We provide them with coaching when we place them in new jobs or give them new challenges or broaden their breadth of responsibility."

Coaches can really help the MVP deal with the inevitable frustrations of acclimatizing to a new position. Barbara Fuchs, Director of Talent Development at UBS Financial Services, comments similarly: "We have cases where it's someone who is excellent and they've been given an even bigger challenge and they just need someone to help them figure out the best way to do it. They're fine-tuning skills that they have already mastered but they just need a little bit of support in one area or the other."

MDS Inc. uses performance coaches to work with new leaders who are about to join a new management team. Coaches work to make sure that the relationship between the new leader and the team works well right from the beginning. Jim Reid, MDS's Executive Vice President of Global Human Resources, recounts how coaching was used in this way when a new CEO joined the company: "I worked with our CEO to say, 'Look, let's get these coaches in to work with you, to interview all the team members and to facilitate a two-day session to make sure that we know what your expectations are and how to work with you. We can lay out our priorities for the first six to twelve months and save ourselves a lot of time and effort.' Since then, we've used this approach in an integrated way probably ten or fifteen times in the last few years."

At Procter & Gamble, individual coaching provided by external consultants is of particular value for MVPs who are entering more senior positions because of the stability of the company's workforce. As Keith Lawrence explains, "P&G is a bit unique. We are one of the few 'build from within' companies in existence today. We don't often bring in outsiders for senior levels. This means that people will have spent several years just within Procter & Gamble when they reach these senior levels. So how do we get external viewpoints and fresh perspectives about the development needs senior leaders might have? This is where we use external coaches. The coaches also provide a safer environment to help them hear some of the tough feedback that they may not have heard."

Some organizations enlist the aid of coaches to meet multiple MVP needs. Canada's cable giant Rogers Communications, for example, uses coaches for skills development but also, as Kevin Pennington explains, "to help people develop their business acumen and to teach MVPs how to navigate the organization. MVPs are not always assigned to a manager who is a good role model for them, so we bring in a coach to work with them." And Ellen Moore explains that Chubb Canada "uses coaching for three different purposes":

> Sometimes we use it when someone is on the cusp of making a major transition into a new role that requires new skills. We believe that a person can be successful if we give him or her some additional support.
>
> We use it sometimes for what I would call early alert. This is when someone whom we believe can be successful, starts hitting

a couple of bumps in the road. So we bring in a coach to work with that person.

Finally, we use it if an excellent performer in the past, now has an issue that requires coaching support.

Moore also mentions a fourth purpose that is clearly new and still emerging. "The leadership team has seen the CEO of the Canadian company successfully use a coach. Now we're getting more requests from our high-potential staff about external and executive coaching as part of the development process, and as part of their own life plan. It's interesting because people are prepared to make a personal commitment, whether that's shared cost or doing their coaching on a Saturday." Coaching in this context is less about meeting specific needs than about developing MVPs generally and for the long term.

Many organizations, however, continue to provide MVPs with individual coaching only on an as-needed basis. As Daniel Sonsino, at Raytheon, confides: "It's really only something that we offer to individuals where it makes sense. We spend a lot of time on the front end to make sure that coaching is targeted toward developmental gaps. Coaching may not always be the solution to the development need. So we spend a good amount of time identifying with that leader why he or she feels coaching is important and necessary." Mark Bornemann describes a similar situation at LoJack: "We use coaching when we believe that someone can add more value to the company. We do this when a person needs a little more guidance and we don't have somebody internally who has the skill set to get them there. We use it more on an as-needed basis for those who will benefit the most from it."

On-the-Job Development

There is no better teacher than experience, but the best teachers usually plan their lessons carefully. As part of a comprehensive integrated plan, on-the-job development typically entails exposing MVPs to a carefully designed program of job experiences. This can involve setting MVPs to work on a succession of projects or placing them in a succession of jobs that broaden their thinking and competencies. In this case, coaching is often provided by internal managers or HR people. External coaches are also sometimes assigned the role discussed in the previous section – helping the MVP adjust to a new job. When it is a component of a comprehensive development program, on-the-job development is a planned activity determined by the role or roles that supervisors would like the MVP to grow into.

Many of the executives I interviewed identify job experience as the single most important contributor to MVP development. "We do believe that on-the-job learning is of higher value than classroom experience," says Laurie Cowan of CSL Behring. Debi King of MDS Nordion goes further: "We certainly believe firmly that the best development occurs on the job. The biggest part of everyone's development has been challenging work assignments and diverse work assignments and involvement in projects that are outside of the scope of their normal job, and international assignments." Wendy Watson, Executive Vice President of Global Services at State Street Corporation, comments similarly but also sees coaching playing a role: "The fastest way to develop someone in my opinion is on-the-job experience where they are actually working on different assignments with different people in different global locations. You probably need a mentor or a coach to work with them to make sure that the development is happening."

Given the importance organizations place on job experience, most stress the hard thinking that goes into placing MVPs optimally. At Procter & Gamble, Keith Lawrence reports, "We spend a tremendous amount of time thinking about what is the right next assignment for the individual." Mark Bornemann notes that at LoJack, "We place a lot of focus on creating job moves for MVPs as part of their development," while Kevin Pennington reports that at Rogers Communications "a great deal of attention is given to getting them involved in the business."

What stands out is the sheer variety of ways and means that organizations use as they seek to broaden their MVPs' job experiences. CSL Behring focuses on project work, both within the MVP's job and outside of it: "We do a pretty good job of forming global project teams and looking for people to take on these opportunities," says Laurie Cowan. Often, as at LoJack, exposing MVPs to new experiences involves sending them abroad. Says Mark Bornemann: "Last year we focused on six or seven people who were really considered MVPs. We were able to send one person over to Italy with his family to become a Managing Director of our Italian operation. We moved another one to Canada to be a General Manager." Keith Lawrence of Procter & Gamble describes broadening the experience of MVPs by moving them to "another region" or assigning them to work "on a major acquisition or in a troubled business unit. These are great 'accelerator experiences' for these individuals." And Vas Nair describes the learning opportunities arising from Schering-Plough's strong growth: "We look for ways to expand on-the-job development opportunities of our top talent. In a company that's growing dramatically, the opportunities for professional growth are always there. We continuously encourage our people to take on global assignments, secondments, and cross-functional project work. This approach has further helped build a · *global, shared accountability* mindset at Schering Plough."

Taken together, the five development activities I have been discussing make up a powerful and thorough program for developing MVPs. Not all companies include all of these activities in their development initiatives. But most include at least three or four. Most also assign a role to coaching, whether formal or informal, internal or external, in each of the development activities undertaken. Coaching is clearly moving far beyond its traditional function of providing remedial aid to troubled performers. Organizations are now making it central to the integrated development programs of their Most Valuable Performers.

Checklist for Creating an Integrated Development Program for MVPs

❑ Work with a coach to create a comprehensive long-term development plan based on a sound assessment of the MVP's strengths, weaknesses, and potential.

❑ Provide opportunities for rigorous formal training involving exposure to senior leaders and subject experts.

❑ Involve your MVPs in action team learning projects that stretch their thinking and capabilities. Make sure the projects are of real significance to the organization. Assign a senior leader to oversee the project and use coaches to provide support.

❑ Provide your MVP with individual, focused, one-on-one development support by assigning him or her an internal or external coach.

❑   Ensure that your MVPs develop on the job by exposing them
     to a variety of job experiences. Provide them with different
     responsibilities. Move them into different jobs. Move them
     to different locations. Take all these steps with a view to the
     roles you would like your MVPs to grow into.

CHAPTER 5

Coaching MVPs and High-Potentials

Coaching in general is a broad-ranging activity that can take place at many levels of the organization. MVP coaching, by contrast, is a highly specialized function that focuses on a very narrow range of people: the 5 to 10 percent of employees who deliver exceptional value to the organization. As employees who constantly seek to improve their own performance as well as that of the organization, MVPs are particularly open to being coached. But, as individuals who aren't afraid to challenge existing ways of thinking and acting, who, in other words, know their own minds, MVPs can also present some unique coaching challenges and opportunities. As we have seen in Chapter 4, MVP coaching can be provided as a stand-alone intervention or as an essential element of a comprehensive, integrated development program. This chapter will focus on MVP coaching itself. It will consider what both MVPs and high-potentials need from coaching and what kind of coaches coach them.

What MVPs Need from Coaching

Why is coaching MVPs different? Paul Larson, an executive coach and Coaching Market Leader for Right Management in Southern California, offers a preliminary view. MVPs, he says, differ not so much in kind as by degree. Larson points to three characteristics that "show up in all coaching engagements" but that are "accentuated with MVPs":

First, there is always some level of self-awareness that needs to be explored and that they want to build on.

Second, there is always a need to improve their understanding of the impact of their behavior on other people.

Third, there is always room to improve their clarity of the expectations, whether from above or what they expect from their own people.

"MVPs," Larson adds by way of explanation, "are generally more motivated than others." Knowing that business performance is intimately connected with their awareness of themselves, of their impact on others, and of the expectations others place on them, they are especially keen to heighten their awareness in such areas. The MVP will do whatever it takes to improve.

The interviews I conducted for this book in large part confirmed Paul Larson's sense of what distinguishes the coaching of MVPs. They also, however, revealed some additional areas of distinction. My list of the key differences in working with and coaching MVPs is as follows:

- They have a high degree of self-awareness and self-understanding
- They often underestimate their ability
- They need feedback
- They are very learning-oriented and want to keep learning and growing
- They are impatient in their drive for results

Let's examine each of these characteristics in turn.

They Have a High Degree of Self-Awareness and Self-Understanding

One sure sign of accomplishment is knowing what you don't know. MVPs are highly self-aware. They have a firm understanding of their strengths but also of their weaknesses – the areas they need to develop. Arabelle Fedora, Coaching Market Leader for the Southern United States at Right Management, confirms their "high degree of self-awareness" and calls them "a coach's dream because they are so receptive to coaching. They don't see themselves as perfect by any stretch of the imagination." According to Right Management's Dina Lichtman,

Senior Vice President, Career Management Consulting, MVPs "tend to be very motivated and very driven. They have good emotional intelligence, which means they really do understand what goes on externally as well as inside themselves and they quickly understand that coaching is about acting upon changes that are beneficial to them and the organization." How, then, do you contribute to the self-knowledge of those who are already self-aware?

Their self-awareness actually makes MVPs particularly receptive to coaching. Coaching can help MVPs build on their self-awareness to become even more valuable to the organization. As Bill Roiter, Managing Partner of MVP Research, comments: "With MVPs, the focus is on continuing to build awareness, as opposed to identifying problem behaviors. It's about helping them to understand what they'd like to change and helping them to look at people who are good in the areas where they want to change."

They Often Underestimate their Own Ability

Despite their self-awareness in most respects, MVPS are often very humble about their own capabilities and often underestimate just how talented they are and what value they bring to the organization. MVPs are very hard on themselves, reports Denise Lockaby, Director of Professional Development at The Stride Rite Corporation. Arabelle Fedora concurs: "They tend to underrate and underestimate their ability. They are very open to improving themselves and to growing." Helping MVPs acquire a more realistic understanding of their value can be an important coaching function.

What is at stake, it's important to see, isn't ego inflation, but even higher levels of performance. MVPs can sometimes be held back by an exaggerated sense of their limitations. Bill Roiter cites the example of "a very successful and highly valued person" he was once asked to coach "who was at the peak of her performance."

> I was puzzled when we started working together. I knew how good she was from what other people had told me. We did some 360 assessments and the results were fabulous. However, her ratings for herself were lower than the others and in some areas they were significantly lower. During our feedback sessions I realized that she lacked confidence and did not realize just how

good she was. She would often focus on self-doubt. As we talked, she was stunned that others thought she was so good at her job. She told me that all her family were high achievers and successful, and when she measured herself against these family members, she doubted her capabilities. The purpose of the coaching was to help her think about her current strengths and how she might add further value to the organization. I got her to imagine herself as a confident person and to behave and think as though she really was confident. It worked wonders for her.

Ed Piccolino, President of Piccolino Associates, LLC, and adjunct coach at Right Management, tells a similar story. He recalls coaching a very high-performing and talented CFO who came across as very introverted and unassuming. The Board wanted to know if he had the potential to be a CEO. Because he didn't light up the room, they weren't sure of his potential:

> It became clear during the course of my assessment that this man was the embodiment of Jim Collins's work on 'Good to Great.' He had extraordinary humility and incredible persistence, in addition to many other fine leadership qualities. But charisma certainly was not one of them. The coaching process gave him a reassuring vote of confidence. And then, with this in mind, he decided, 'I'm going for the corner office, whether it's here or someplace else.' Both the Board and the CEO were delighted with his thinking. In order to develop and retain him so that one day he could be considered on a level playing field with other candidates for the CEO role, they kept him in his role but gave him an important operating piece of the company's business to run in addition.

As both Piccolino's and Roiter's stories demonstrate, bolstering the confidence of MVPs can play a key role in spurring them on to greater success.

They Need Feedback

Providing MVPs with feedback goes hand in hand with helping them further their self-awareness. Ed Piccolino and Jim Reid, Executive Vice President of Global Human Resources at MDS Inc., both report that MVPs don't simply wait for feedback to come to them. They are voracious in actively looking for feedback and acting on it once they have it. Daniel Sonsino, Senior Manager of Talent Management and Succession Planning at Raytheon, identifies the younger generation of high-potentials as being in particular need of feedback: "The high-potentials in our younger generation have a need for immediate and tangible feedback. They are different from the older generations." Feedback provides MVPs with benchmarks to assess how well they are doing and whether or not they are achieving the required results. Feedback is essential for building their confidence and for identifying areas for further development. They need feedback, not only because they represent the young and impatient but because they often do not know how their behaviour impacts others.

A recent poll by PDI, Inc.: "High-performing individuals are used to success but often don't take the time to consider how it is achieved or how their actions impact others," said PDI's David Peterson, Ph.D., senior vice president, executive coaching services. "They assume that what they are doing today to produce results will continue to serve them well going forward, without realizing that they are failing to build the strong relationships and loyalty that will actually enhance their chances for long-term success. Coaching is one of the best ways to make sure they learn what they need to deliver results long-term as well as short-term."[1]

They are Very Learning-Oriented and Want to Keep Learning and Growing

"The good news," says Ed Piccolino, "is that MVPs are very highly motivated. Once they get feedback, even if it's negative, they act on it. They want to learn. They want to get better – always. They just can't move quickly enough or intensely enough. In fact, one of the challenges in working with them is that you really have to be aligned with them in their mindset."

In Bill Roiter's view, you actually have to slow them down. Learning, he points out, involves reflection as well as action: "So one of the things I've learned with MVPs is to restrict them from acting immediately because once they get feedback they go off and

---

1 PR Newswire (press release) - New York, NY, USA.

implement the changes. That's OK because they usually will do it well. But for them to learn, I need to get them to ponder a little bit, which they'll do if they're given the time."

Roiter cites the example of coaching a "senior and successful person" who was being groomed for an even higher senior position.

> Some of the feedback he received was that he wasn't overly people-oriented and that some people had difficulty interacting with him. He was not as smooth as he thought as he was. He had been in the job for three years, had come from another company, but he still felt that he was new to the job and didn't own it. Thus he didn't always feel comfortable when interacting with the people around him, both in meetings and informally. I asked him to notice 'how other people interact with each other, not with you but with each other,' and told him, 'Next time we meet we'll talk about what you saw.' What I was purposefully doing was building his awareness of interpersonal relationships and behavior. Once MVPs are aware that they are not as good at something as they could be, they immediately want to know the solution – 'How am I going to fix this?' So change becomes a mandate. It's not something they have to do because of outside pressure but because they see that they need to do it.

Unlike coaching others, coaching the MVP, in short, requires knowing how to apply the brakes as well as the accelerator. The same is true in dealing with their drive for results.

They are Impatient in their Drive for Results

One of the unique challenges of coaching MVPs is dealing with their drive and their impatience not just to learn but to deliver actual business results. "The MVPs that I have coached," reports Lanoix, "have an incredible drive for results. They're incredibly motivated and they are on a high about winning almost all the time. They have a vision and they just move in that direction." While this drive for results is undeniably a great strength, it can also sometimes create difficulties for MVPs. Denise Lockaby of The Stride Rite Corporation finds that "our high-potentials or MVPs are very hard on themselves. They want success and they want it now. They are not long on patience." Being very hard on yourself isn't always a prescription for maximizing your performance. Sometimes, when coaching the MVP, the drive for results needs to be tempered.

Ed Piccolino gives an example of coaching an MVP employed in a Fortune 100 company whose drive for results threatened his proper development.

> The COO asked me to work with this person. We gave him a key job assignment that was a stretch for him. We sent him to manage a key business in Latin America and this gave him an opportunity to have a fantastic junior general management role. Now here is my point illustrating impatience. About six months after he had been in the new job, he called me and said, 'I have done this job, now what's next?' Not to mention the challenges associated with all kinds of cultural and internal equity issues such impatience can trigger. We had to make sure that he continued to do that job for a while longer and to keep learning and developing – if for no other reason than to really take his measure performance-wise. Fortunately, he really did a great job and the company did a brilliant job, really, of lining up well-conceived (i.e., aggressive/ stretch) follow-on assignments for him. He ultimately went on to a spectacular career that created literally billions of shareholder value. I can't think of a more stellar success story.

The spectacular career he went on to was to become the CEO of the firm itself. Of course, one of the keys to his success was receiving coaching for his drive and impatience.

Who Coaches MVPs?

If MVPs present unique coaching challenges and opportunities, who are the coaches currently tasked with meeting MVP needs? Coaching the MVP is a multi-faceted enterprise performed not just by "coaches" *per se* but by people in a host of different positions both inside and outside of the organization. In many organizations, for example, managers are expected to act as coaches to their employees. They develop their talent as a normal part of their management role. This section will look at who coaches the MVPs.

As we saw in the previous chapter, coaches come in many forms:

- Managers
- Human Resources departments

- MVPs who coach others
- Manager-mentors
- Internal coaches
- External coaches

Managers

Many organizations rely heavily on managers to provide coaching. "Typically," says Wendy Watson, Executive Vice President, Global Services of State Street Corporation, "the coaching comes from the person's boss or a senior person from another business unit." Watson's comment is itself typical of the statements I heard from many executives interviewed for this book. "We tell our managers that they need to coach and develop their people," says Brian Chitester, Vice President of Organization Development and People Capability at PepsiCo International." And Debi King, Senior Vice President of Human Resources at MDS Nordion, observes: "We expect every leader to coach their people and everyone's supposed to get some form of coaching from their boss. What I like about this approach to coaching is that it develops the executives as they coach others. It also gives the people in the talent pool the opportunity to interact with one of these executives."

We will take a closer look at the role of manager as coach, including training that can be provided to help managers be successful coaches, in Chapter 9.

Human Resources

As we will see in Chapter 8, the role of Human Resources departments in the coaching process is usually to act as the overall facilitator; however, some HR departments also provide coaching itself. We will talk about HR's role as coach in more detail in Chapter 8.

MVPs who Coach Others

One of the companies I interviewed takes an innovative approach to coaching their MVPs and high-potential employees. They ask MVPs themselves to coach talented individuals still at the level below them: "We use the people who are in our executive talent pool as coaches to the talent pools below them," explains MDS Nordion's Debi King. "This is part of their development and we ensure that coaching is one of their core skills. MVPs get external coaching and then are expected to coach people below them. We have two people right now whom we're actually putting through a very intense coaching certification program."

MVPs both further the development of those below them and, in the process, further their own development. This approach takes full advantage of one of the key defining characteristics of MVPs that I mentioned at the very beginning of the book – that MVPs serve as role models who seek to develop the skills of their less successful peers. In enlisting MVPs as coaches, MDS Inc. draws on one of their defining strengths.

Manager-Mentors

In addition to providing coaching, some organizations also provide MVPs with mentors. While mentors can perform some of the functions usually associated with coaching, they also serve as sounding boards and trusted advisors. Mentors are typically experienced internal people well versed in the business, social, and political dynamics of the organization. They can help MVPs manage their way around the company or get advice on how to do their job. Normally, a mentor works in areas not directly related to the MVP's sphere and can therefore provide independent advice. Mentors may be assigned to people, or they may join a roster of volunteer mentors. Sometimes organizations have a formal mentoring program that is based on a clearly defined process; in other cases the mentoring may take place on an as-needed basis. Some companies provide their mentors with training.

Wendy Watson of State Street advances the case for mentoring in general:

> It is helpful to be able to go and talk to somebody who doesn't have a vested interest in your own personal situation. You may need someone to talk to about a situation in an open and honest way. You might say to the mentor, 'Here is this situation and

this is how I responded. I don't think I handled it very well, what do you think?' It's helpful to talk to someone who knows the company, knows the political environment, and is independent of where you are in the organization. They can listen to you and say, 'You know, I think you really screwed up. Did you think of this, did you think of that?' and maybe even help with some counsel in terms of remedial things. It's pretty easy for an executive to get off track through some really unfortunate and often trivial mistake. Being able to identify that and get some help in terms of how to do it next time is very helpful. It's probably easier to do it with somebody who isn't in your own business area.

As these comments suggest, mentoring can often help MVPs problem solve and deal with workplace stresses in general. The mentor is there for an MVP to consult as issues arise.

A second, more focused style of mentoring is also possible. At MDS Nordion, as Debi King explains, mentoring is used to address specific development needs: "In addition to providing our MVPs with coaches, we provide them with internal mentors. We use people who are already on the executive team. They work with people who are one level below. These mentors are people who we feel have the strength in the areas where an MVP has development needs. An example would be where our VP of Sales and Marketing is mentoring our leader of R&D in order to develop his or her commercial acumen."

In much the same way as they provide training for coaches, organizations sometimes offer training for mentors. Michael Lindemann, recalls creating such a training program while at a well known global company: "We gave our mentors two full days of intensive training which I had custom created and which I personally delivered. Then I would regularly follow up to see how things were going for both the mentor and the person being mentored."

Internal Coaches

Many of the companies interviewed use both internal and external coaches. Some prefer internal coaches because of their familiarity with the organization's dynamics. As Bob Levenson, Director of Global Talent Development at Millipore Corporation, explains: "Internal coaches know the total environment in which their clients operate – their peers, the business pressures they face, the unique aspects of the culture, etcetera."

Internal coaches, normally drawn from management or from HR, may be used in a variety of ways. Sometimes, as at Raytheon, they are used to coach people at more junior levels: "For our emerging talent we actually use internal coaches whom we've certified through a program that we developed," says Raytheon's Sonsino. At other times, as at UBS Financial Services, internal coaches can be used as career development coaches. Michelle Blieberg explains: "We have a number of internal coaches – HR or business people who play the role of inside career coaches. In the beginning of our leadership development process, everybody was assigned an internal coach. Now we realize we don't need to do that. We advertise that we have it and when people need to talk to someone in confidence, we've got line managers in each of the regions who are assigned to play this role."

Bob Hedley of Maple Leaf Foods describes precisely what internal career coaching has to offer: "It's about giving somebody the opportunity to develop by examining their career goals and aspirations. A lot of people struggle at defining what it is they actually want to do and what mountain they want to climb. So a developmental coach can help with that. We find that feedback very useful and supportive. Effective managers who act as performance coaches also help in terms of keeping a person focused on delivering outstanding results in a values consistent way."

External Coaches

Organizations tend to reserve the use of external coaches for their senior and high-potential people. At Raytheon, says Daniel Sonsino, "all of our coaches are external for our director level and above," while at PepsiCo International, says Brian Chitester, "we use external coaches for the highest potential folks." At Schering-Plough, Vas Nair notes that coaches are retained "for the more senior groups, more often than not vice presidents and above," while Meg Jones notes that The Children's Hospital of Philadelphia finds external coaches for individuals "who are emerging leaders and/or identified for accelerated development."

External coaches offer coachees confidentiality and in some cases a broader skill set than any internal coach can offer. Debi King describes the practice at MDS Nordion: "For the people in the acceleration pool development plan we've hooked them up with an external coach. And we did that because we felt we wanted it to be something where there were no inhibitions." Bob Hedley of Maple Leaf Foods stresses the developmental support external coaches can offer: "Where we will use external coaching is for specific developmental gaps. So if I've got a vice president or even a president or a director who says, 'This person has a real hard developmental need and there's some urgency in it,' and there's a feeling that coaching is the right way to go, we will contract with a professional coach and do a diagnostic and a more in-depth intervention in those situations." "Coaching is based on development needs," says Schering-Plough's Nair. "The idea is to look at our top talent in relation to our critical skill sets. Where appropriate, these individuals partner with executive coaches to achieve their development objectives."

For those organizations that emphasize development, external coaches tend to be used selectively. "We will use coaches selectively, depending on their development needs," says Meg Jones of The Children's Hospital of Philadelphia. Naomi Shaw reports similarly for Scotiabank: "I would say we use it very selectively. For example, we have coaches who we use for presentation skills and we've even had situations where a manager of an MVP is running into a challenging coaching situation with that person. We engage a coach to support that manager in being a more effective coach. They still have the responsibility for working with their direct report but they're getting some support and guidance kind of behind the scenes."

The relationship of the MVP's manager to the coach is an important concern for some organizations. The reason Scotiabank is selective in its use of external coaches, explains Naomi Shaw, is that "we are very cognizant of not taking away responsibility from managers in their role as the coach. What we don't want to do is run into situations where managers who are not good coaches want us to hire an external coach for their direct report to compensate for the fact that they're not doing it." More positively, Brian Chitester points that retaining an external coach can have benefits for managers and the organization: "Engaging coaches has some ancillary effects on managers, as they start to learn the coach is coaching their people and it helps build their own coaching skills."

David Denison, President and CEO of the Canada Pension Plan Investment Board, expresses another concern some organizations have about engaging an external coach: "When we do use external coaches, the corporation in effect hires the coach and is responsible for the outcomes. The engagement is not owned by the individual. I will interview the coaches as well as the coachee. I tell the person who will be coached, 'This engagement is going to be a corporate engagement for this resource. It's not going to be your engagement. Just to make it clear that the reason we're doing this is to help make you more effective in your role within CPP Investment Board. It is not a personal agenda that you have here.' There needs to be strong accountability back to me for what the results are around the work that the coach will be doing with the individual." We will be looking at organizing external coaching for MVPs in more detail in Chapter 7.

* * *

MVPs are unique members of any organization. The very characteristics that make them the organization's highest performers also single them out as having unique development and coaching needs. Among other traits, their self-awareness, their burning desire to learn and improve, and their drive for results and success call for a complex and multi-faceted coaching approach. As we have seen, organizations are relying on a number of different sources to provide coaching – not just external coaches but internal coaches, managers, mentors, and even other MVPs. Each has a specific and important contribution to make to ensuring MVP development and success.

While our focus so far has been on enhancing success for MVPs, it would be foolhardy to ignore the fact that MVPs, especially those who are newly brought in from another company, do sometimes risk failing. In the next chapter, Chapter 6, my colleague Dominick Volini offers his insights into the valuable role that coaching plays in assisting externally recruited MVPs who have reached a crisis point.

Summary

- MVPs present unique coaching challenges and opportunities:

  * They have a high degree of self-awareness and self-understanding
  * They often underestimate their own ability
  * They need feedback
  * They are very learning-oriented and want to keep learning and growing
  * They are impatient in their drive for results

- Coaching MVPs is a complex activity requiring intervention from a variety of coaching sources:

  * Managers
  * Human Resources departments
  * MVPs who coach others
  * Manager-mentors
  * Internal coaches
  * External coaches

CHAPTER 6

Coaching the Failing MVP

Dominick Volini, Ph.D.
Northeast Leadership Development Practice Lead,
Right Management

As was emphasized in Chapter 4, coaching has moved well beyond its traditional function as an aid to the struggling person. It has been shown to add significant value to development initiatives of all kinds, especially when they target MVPs. MVPs, however, are as human as the rest of us. They, too, sometimes struggle and face failure. Typically, the MVP is most at risk when he or she is brought into an organization from the outside to assume a leadership role. In fact, research has shown that fully 40 percent of all newly appointed leaders fail to meet the expectations of their organization.[1] In such instances, coaching of a more traditional kind can play a valuable role in righting a listing ship. For this chapter, Margaret Butteriss has asked me to draw on my coaching experiences to talk about externally recruited MVPs who are failing. I will consider the reasons why externally recruited MVPs fail, and point out ways to prevent MVPs from failing in their new positions. In particular, I will focus on how coaching can be used to bring the MVP back on track after a crisis point has been reached. Throughout the chapter, I will be illustrating my thinking by referring to the details of a particular coaching assignment, which is described below.

Why do Externally Recruited MVPs Fail?

Recently, I picked up a voice-mail message from the HR representative of a medium-sized, moderately successful local service industry

---

1 Right Management "New Leader Coaching" 2004.

provider that sounded like a fairly routine request – a Senior Vice President was in need of coaching. However, when I called back, the HR representative gave me a much more complex story. The request was for coaching to help a floundering external hire, a Senior VP of Analytics and Strategy who had been brought aboard to revolutionize the way business decisions were made in the company. Up until then, the firm had prided itself on promoting from within, and most managers, all the way up to the CEO, had grown up in the business and had their own well-entrenched approach to the work. Now this new individual had been brought in to establish a data-based analytic department to supply functional managers with information to better define financial and service problems and opportunities. His group was to further provide modeling for alternative solution choice and monitoring of action results, in particular, impact on revenue, profit margin, and service-level ratings. Having arrived with some fanfare, a year later the executive had not delivered on expectations, and had ruffled many feathers while trying to do so.

Why was this MVP failing? It would be too easy to pin the blame solely on him. He certainly wasn't lacking the essential capabilities and skills to achieve success. Almost by definition, MVPs rarely do. When externally hired MVPs fail, it is generally because of mistakes made during the process of selection and the process of assimilation. Margaret Butteriss discussed these mistakes extensively in her previous book, *Corporate MVPs*, co-authored with Bill Roiter.[2] The point I want to emphasize here is that when organizations bring in an external recruit, they often neglect to consider the larger picture. Their focus tends to be on the match between the MVP's specific capabilities and the job's specific requirements. Organizations regularly fail to take into account the cultural skills and expectations that the new recruit carries with him or her from business life in another company that, culturally, may operate in a completely different way.

The particular role that an organization's leadership can play in the failure of a new recruit deserves special attention. The pattern of behavior is depressingly familiar. Leadership:

1. Makes great claims about this new, strategically important position before the person arrives.
2. Sets business goals and expectations for the person without the person's input.

---

2 Margaret Butteriss and Bill Roiter, John Wiley & Sons Canada, Ltd., 2004, pp. 116-123.

3. Does not do due diligence on either the person's background or the organization's receptivity to the new hire.
4. Spends money "freely" on the new department (while others are told to hold down costs).
5. Denies reports of problems early on and says some period of adjustment is normal.
6. Takes no real responsibility for problem escalation.
7. Finally, considers it solely the new hire's "behavioral problem."

Clearly, in cases where such a pattern of dysfunction plays out, leadership, perhaps as much as the MVP, must bear responsibility for a failing performance.

In many cases, in fact, not just leadership but almost the entire organization bears at least some responsibility for an MVP's failure. As in the case of my Analytics and Strategy SVP cited above, some organizations that have little experience in bringing someone in from the outside can be less than receptive when an MVP is finally hired externally. The problem is compounded if leadership's great claims for the position raise unrealistic expectations among the new hire's colleagues and subordinates. The new hire is almost set up for failure. And if others in the organization become convinced that the new hire's department is being showered with money while they are being asked to hold the line, rather than failure being something the people in the organization simply stand by and witness, it may be something they actually collude in.

How to Prevent Externally Recruited MVPs from Failing

MVPs are hired for sound business reasons. They normally offer hard-to-find skill sets, as well unique experience and expertise that are simply not available through internal recruitment. Since their mission is often critical and time is usually short, developing a high-potential candidate internally is rarely viable. Organizations, clearly, have much at stake in ensuring that externally recruited MVPs integrate successfully and realize their full potential.

What, then, can the organization do to prevent the external recruit from failing in the first place? Taking the following steps can reduce the risk of failure considerably:

Preventing Failure

1. Avoid misunderstanding by anticipating character. Understand that people with certain competencies often have stereotypic personality traits, too. Think of how movies and cartoons (*Dilbert*, for example!) depict accountants, engineers, Wall Streeters, and used car salesmen! These are often grossly stereotypical characterizations, but they have a familiar feeling about them, based on our everyday experience when we actually meet people from these disciplines.

2. Conduct a risk analysis along with the usual business benefit analysis done for a strategically critical new hire.

3. Prepare future colleagues for the new hire's potentially different cultural style.

4. Assess the organization's current cultural norms ("how we work around here") for use in a very thorough onboarding process.

5. Assign a culturally wise and organizationally respected mentor to the new hire.

6. Hire a coach from outside who knows the company and the leadership. Set up an expectation of having frequent dialogue with the new hire, the direct supervisor, the supervisor the next level up, and HR (at a minimum).

7. Conduct engagement sessions with the new hire (and the new group, if appropriate) and other key departments.

8. Set realistic goals and track progress.

How to Help the Failing MVP

Externally recruited MVPs sometimes fail when steps like those outlined above haven't been taken and even, occasionally, when they have. Since MVPs are hard to come by, and since they potentially offer enormous benefits to the organization, giving up on them without a fight is a poor option. The organization must and can rectify the situation, especially in instances when it is complicit in an MVP's failure. In practice, many organizations do put up a fight, although sometimes, it has to be said, only after HR advises management that the person needs to be given a chance rather than shown the door.

The signs of MVP failure can be summarized as follows:

- **Results shortfall:** The anticipated business deliverables fall far short of expectations.
- **Group confusion/attrition:** There is confusion and, generally, resultant high attrition in the new manager's group.
- **Peer revolt:** The new manager's peers are complaining bitterly about the way he or she does business.
- **Perfect storm:** A combination of two or all three of the above.

When these signs appear, bringing in an external coach offers one of the most effective means of righting the situation. Coaching in such circumstances has a long and proven track record.

Such coaching, it must be noted, is different from the coaching discussed in other chapters of this book. Since the organization must share some of the blame for MVP failure, the organization, and not just the MVP, must also be coached. Coaches, as a result, have to do more direct work with bosses, peers and subordinates; they have to influence work process changes for the MVP beyond the behavioral changes normal to coaching; and they have to ensure that a mentoring element (a culturally savvy senior leader) is added to the coaching mix. Finally, they must work with HR to institute more rigorous cultural due diligence in the recruiting/hiring/onboarding processes. I've been involved in coaching assignments where bosses have set up weekly reviews of the MVP's work with business unit leaders to assure their co-operation; where the MVP's peers have created cross-functional task teams with the MVP and his/her staff; and where leadership and HR revamped their strategy for bringing in MVPs.

The distinctiveness of remedial coaching is revealed most significantly in four specific stages of the coaching process:

- Diagnosis
- Assessment
- Coaching
- Follow-up

Let's examine each stage in turn.

Diagnosis

As with any coaching engagement, the coach must convene an initial meeting with Human Resources and/or the MVP's supervisor to determine the scope of the work involved. When the assignment calls for remedial coaching, the discussion necessarily concentrates on identifying the problem at hand. Usually, the "problem" presented to the coach rests squarely with the MVP. In the case of my Analytics and Strategy SVP, I was told of a peer group complaint: the new MVP was not inclusive and kept them from making legitimate contributions to his analytics. In response, this peer group found ways not to co-operate with the SVP, and the SVP proved incapable of delivering the promised improvements in decision-making, cost reduction, and service quality. The MVP, according to the client, dealt with his peers in a high-handed manner. Therefore, the premise on which coaching was to proceed was that the MVP needed to change his behavior. He needed to collaborate more effectively with his peers when working on their departmental cost and quality improvement initiatives.

Once the hiring clients have described the scope of work as they see it, remedial coaching of externally hired MVPs must part company with other types of coaching by subjecting this description to extra-careful scrutiny. Coaches should accept the client accounts as legitimate points of view, but they also need to ask probing questions to ensure that the problem as identified by the client is, in fact, the real problem (or the whole problem). Digging deeper and diagnosing carefully before recommending an intervention, coaches must consider the problem within the larger context of the whole system. When learning about the behaviors of the MVP, coaches must learn about and understand the multiple interactions the MVP has with other individuals, departments, and processes. They must also take into account business expectations.

Given the specialized nature of remedial coaching assignments (that is, where the interaction of the MVP with new colleagues and within the structure of a new company culture plays a key role), I recommend asking four sets of questions to get to the root of the problem and define the expected results of the coaching engagement.

First set of questions – responding to the client's presentation of the "problem":

- When was this problem first noticed?
- How has it been brought to the MVP's attention?

- What has been done so far to address it?
- What has been the result of any attempt to fix it?
- What will happen if you do nothing?
- How different is the behavior/attitude of the MVP from the norm here? From the behaviors/attitudes of other specific groups?
- What particular impact is the problem having on the business results? On other groups? On other people?
- How long can the problem go on before it becomes intolerable? Then what?
- What would be a best outcome of coaching? What would be marginally acceptable?
- How soon are results needed/expected?

Second set of questions – setting the problem in the larger organizational context:

- How did the MVP's position become open?
- What was the history of this function prior to the MVP's arrival?
- Tell me about the recruiting process: length, difficulty, internal candidates, and so on?
- Why was this person chosen?
- How were peers and others in the department involved in the selection?
- How was the MVP orientated, onboarded?
- What was the organization told about the MVP's role and goals? Who told them? How was it communicated?

Third set of questions – addressing the MVP's own response to the prospect of being coached and his or her working relationship with others in the organization:

- What has the MVP been told about coaching? What was his/her reaction?
- What is the potential downside of coaching on the MVP?
- What obstacles may be faced in this coaching engagement – for instance, heavy MVP travel, project deadlines, competing development demands, or other issues?
- How will this coaching be positioned and communicated to other significant people?
- How might others have been contributing to this problem? How has that been handled so far?
- How might others react to this coaching?

Fourth set of questions – to be realistic:

- What if coaching doesn't work?
- What is the alternative solution?

When I put these questions to the clients in the case of the Analytics and Strategy SVP, the following facts emerged. The CEO had created the MVP's new role and department to improve service and reduce costs by helping operational leaders to make better business decisions. But there had been little communication to anyone in the organization prior to hiring the MVP. Further, there was little true onboarding – that is, orientation of the MVP to the functional, physical, cultural, and social ways that work was done in this organization, and introducing him to the people he was to work with. The MVP was simply told to expect some mild resistance to him, his role, and his department, but that the CEO would smooth things over. So the new SVP showed up on day one and scheduled a meeting with internal clients to do project planning and introduce his team. He assumed, wrongly, that people at his new company, as at his previous organization, would value this type of internal consultancy. As my questions revealed, the "problem," clearly, was not simply his own – and the organization's blindness to its share of the responsibility only made things worse. In fact, even as my coaching engagement began, the hiring client continued to believe that the MVP would eventually fit in, regardless. Coaching, if successful, would only accelerate the process, in the eyes of the CEO. In other words, the organization remained oblivious to the fact that it, too, would have to change for the MVP to have any chance of succeeding.

Assessment

Assessment is extremely important in the case of an externally recruited MVP who is failing. Among the plethora of assessment tools covered in Chapter 3, the 360-degree interview survey of key people with whom the MVP interacts yields particularly useful insights. The 360-degree survey process offers the most direct means possible of testing the validity and universality of the account of the problem supplied by Human Resources and the MVP's supervisor. It enables the coach to determine how isolated the MVP has become from his/her co-workers or how willing those co-workers are to support the MVP in helpful mentoring ways during and after the coaching engagement. It helps the coach identify stakeholders and gage the problem's effect on them. And it allows the coach to judge how well the organization's various functional groups co-operate in achieving larger business goals, quite apart from the efforts of the MVP. In other words, 360-degree surveying allows the coach to uncover whether organizational problems and dysfunctions having little to do with the MVP may be at play.

While other assessment tools – online surveys, for example – may also serve up useful results, they simply cannot match the wealth of information provided by a 360-degree personal interview process. An online survey is less labor-intensive, but it provides no opportunity to investigate germane topics that emerge unanticipated during the initial scoping session. It also, of course, cannot record the interviewees' facial expressions when they are asked about the MVP. Smiles and grimaces convey important emotional content impossible to access via an online survey. Such secondary information can be invaluable when coaching the MVP about how to work with the person interviewed or that person's team. It is worth reiterating that, unlike in other coaching assignments, in remedial coaching of externally hired MVPs, coaches must investigate the organization as well as the MVP. With the 360-degree interviews, coaches are best equipped to learn more about the interviewees themselves, the cultural norms often missed by new hires, and aspects of the workplace that support or hinder performance but are never addressed directly.

A key question to ask the MVP before the 360-degree process begins is what he or she anticipates the responses from colleagues will be. The MVP's response affords an insight into his or her awareness of and sensitivity to the perceptions of others. Assessing this level of awareness and sensitivity will provide the coach with guidance when deciding on the type and level of coaching required.

How are the people to be interviewed identified? Ask the MVP:

- In this organization, who do you work most closely with to establish strategy and business plans, or who do you partner with on deliverables?
- Who do you or your group provide services for, and who do you or your group receive input from?
- Who are your internal clients? Who are your external clients, and would it be appropriate to interview them?
- What other key stakeholders or influential people are there in the organization that are not already identified?

In answering such questions, the MVP himself or herself will provide the coach with a comprehensive list of appropriate people to interview.

How did the assessment process work out with my Analytics and Strategy SVP? He was very accepting and seemed genuinely pleased to have coaching assistance. In his previous organization, coaching was viewed as a perk. He admitted to not attending to the issue that had led up to this coaching proposal. The issue, he explained, escaped his attention because of his focus on organizing his team, his deliverables, and his new life after moving across the country. He quickly listed people to contact but was less sure about their response to questions. In all, this was a journey into new territory for him, but he was optimistic and looking forward to getting into it. We also agreed on several personality instruments to round out the feedback and to help inform a specific development plan for coaching.

Coaching

I have already spoken at some length about what remedial coaching itself involves and how it differs from other kinds of coaching. I would here like to include a few additional comments.

First, coaches must work with coachees to persuade them to acknowledge the urgency of the issue and to seek a timely resolution. In cases where remedial coaching is required – unlike in cases requiring developmental coaching – the business performance of the MVP, and by extension the organization, is being adversely affected *now*. The sooner a remedy is found, the better. The very first step in finding a remedy rests with the MVP, who must acknowledge the need for urgent change.

Second, once coaches have gained such an acknowledgement from coachees, they must further press coachees to enter into a closer working relationship (at least for a while) with the boss, a mentor, and perhaps the Human Resources department. Coaches must also, of course, ensure that these stakeholders sign on, too. MVPs in crisis need the support of superiors who can lend the MVPs authority when they need it; of mentors who can provide insight into the very cultural and political issues within the organization that may be dragging the MVPs down; and of HR, the organizational function that has the greatest experience and competence in dealing with performance issues.

Third, once coaching sessions begin, bosses, peers, and subordinates, as well as the coachee, should take part together in pairs ·in at least some of the sessions. As I said earlier, in remedial coaching, uniquely, the coach's task is to coach the organization as well as the MVP. The inclusion of bosses, peers, and subordinates provides the surest means of practicing such broadly aimed coaching. Since miscommunication and misunderstanding often play a significant role in MVP failure, bringing the MVP together with other stakeholders in the controlled and structured environment of a coaching session can go a fair way towards resolving the crisis. It also sets up a model for how they can successfully work together beyond the coaching engagement.

Fourth, because remedial coaching involves greater urgency, the frequency of coaching sessions, during the first three months at any rate, should be greater than in developmental coaching. Sessions should be held every week instead of every second week. Furthermore, the sessions should focus on the MVP's functional task performance, along with more general leadership or skills development. In other words, addressing performance issues should remain the center of attention throughout the coaching engagement.

Having brought such considerations to bear on my coaching of the Analytics and Strategy SVP, I'm happy to report that the results were generally positive. The SVP learned to be more patient with internal customers, explaining his process and the potential positive impact on their work. In turn, peers become more comfortable with his collaboration. This led to more positive business results, which made everyone more confident in the new function and in the MVP. The boss and MVP both now feel more secure.

Follow-up

The task of remedial coaching is far from complete once the reasons for MVP failure have been identified and resolved. The coach must also work with the coachee and the organization at large to ensure that problems don't re-emerge. The coachee must be encouraged, perhaps with the aid of some structured review program, to remain vigilant. He or she must periodically ask trusted colleagues and HR, "How's it going? What are you hearing?" Quarterly meetings with the boss should also be arranged to review results and candidly discuss what is working well and what is not. Coaches should assist in creating Service

Level Agreements between coaches and their internal customers. These agreements should include formal reviews of what is working well and what is not. Coaches should make sure that MVPs enter into and maintain a mentor relationship with a senior leader. MVPs should also be encouraged to socialize with colleagues to the extent that is normal within the organization. By following these steps at the urging of coaches, MVPs and their organizations can go a long way towards securing the gains achieved by remedial coaching.

A final word of advice to pass on to the MVP: Nothing beats looking in the mirror and asking yourself, "Am I doing well?" Trust your gut. If you think something is askew, chase it down by asking others to validate or debunk your hunch.

Is Coaching Worth it?

Coaching, especially remedial coaching, is labor-intensive. It requires a considerable investment of money by the organization and of time by individuals who have a stake in the outcome. Coaching, as a result, may not on the face of it seem worthwhile. A company may believe we think wrongly that it might be better off simply axing the failing MVP and moving on.

But consider these arguments to the contrary. MVPs, precisely because they are MVPs, are usually hired for pressing strategic reasons that are always time-sensitive. Axing an MVP, therefore, incurs not only the cost of replacing him or her (generally figured at 2.5 times salary at an executive level), but also the costs associated with delaying the achievement of the business strategy the MVP was hired to drive in the first place. In other words, lost opportunity costs, as well as replacement costs, must be figured into the cost/value ratio. The financial fallout can be dramatic, even traumatic. By contrast, a successful coaching outcome, besides delivering the business results expected, ensures that the MVP becomes a vital contributing member of leadership. Further, even if coaching does not result in retention of a particular MVP, the organization stands to gain insight into successfully onboarding MVPs in future, thus saving money and accelerating time to achieve optimum performance. Coaching may have its costs, but its benefits are overwhelming.

When to Admit Defeat

Not all situations are rectifiable. Not all MVPs can recover. Sometimes the hole dug by the MVP and the organization is just too deep. A fresh start would be quicker for business results. But how can HR and senior management know when that point has been reached? The presence of one or more of the following signs should give management pause:

- After, say, one month of work, the boss, the MVP or other key stakeholders show reluctance to give the coaching full effort.
- Initially successful change only leads to additional problems involving the original business decision for the MVP's role or the execution of the strategy.
- After some initial assessment, the MVP demonstrates an inability to either perform the task or truly fit in with the culture.

I am familiar with the case of a younger, highly talented individual who was hired in desperation after many months of searching. She was acknowledged to be a stretch hire but had the basics. The coach was called when her staff kept complaining about her management style and her internal customers felt she was a bit pretentious. At first, the coaching went well and people calmed down. But then she made some fundamentally poor business decisions that were not coaching-related. Leadership could no longer support her, and the decision was made to terminate her. MVPs can fail.

Tough business decisions affecting people's careers have to be made every day. Telling MVPs, who characteristically hate to fail, that an engagement just isn't working is never easy. The main thing to emphasize is that it's not personal. Blame can almost always be shared around.

* * *

This chapter has considered the instance of the externally recruited MVP who fails to meet expectations and the role of coaching in helping him or her to get back on track. As I have argued, organizations would do best to avoid problems in the first place by recognizing the cultural challenges often facing a new hire and having a formal on-boarding process in place before the hire is made. Once an MVP is in place and a problem has arisen, remedial coaching is often the best answer. In such cases, the coach must coach the organization as well as the MVP. The coach must take care to diagnose the problem accurately, assess both the MVP and the organization's cultural milieu, involve all stakeholders in intensive and urgent coaching sessions, and take measures to ensure that new problems do not arise after the coaching engagement ends. While remedial coaching can make heavy demands on everyone involved, MVPs and all they have to offer are worth the investment.

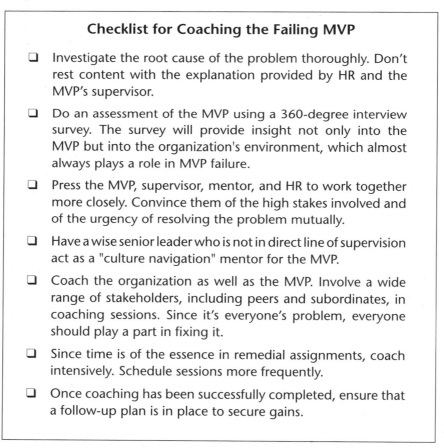

Checklist for Coaching the Failing MVP

❏ Investigate the root cause of the problem thoroughly. Don't rest content with the explanation provided by HR and the MVP's supervisor.

❏ Do an assessment of the MVP using a 360-degree interview survey. The survey will provide insight not only into the MVP but into the organization's environment, which almost always plays a role in MVP failure.

❏ Press the MVP, supervisor, mentor, and HR to work together more closely. Convince them of the high stakes involved and of the urgency of resolving the problem mutually.

❏ Have a wise senior leader who is not in direct line of supervision act as a "culture navigation" mentor for the MVP.

❏ Coach the organization as well as the MVP. Involve a wide range of stakeholders, including peers and subordinates, in coaching sessions. Since it's everyone's problem, everyone should play a part in fixing it.

❏ Since time is of the essence in remedial assignments, coach intensively. Schedule sessions more frequently.

❏ Once coaching has been successfully completed, ensure that a follow-up plan is in place to secure gains.

CHAPTER 7

Organizing External Coaching for the MVP

As we have seen in earlier chapters, MVPs receive coaching from a variety of sources, both formal and informal, both inside the organization and out. In this chapter, I will be narrowing my focus to consider the coaching of MVPs by external coaches. How do organizations typically choose external coaches to meet the needs of their MVPs? How do they make sure that the aims of coaches are aligned with the aims of the organization? How are coaches matched with MVPs? And once coaching begins, what might the process look like? By addressing these questions, this chapter will be outlining an effective regime for the coaching of MVPs by external coaches. Subjects covered will include:

- Choosing a coach – what to look for
- Creating a coaching pool
- Orienting the coach to the company
- Matching coach and coachee
- The coaching process – what to expect

Choosing a Coach – What to Look For

What characteristics make for an ideal MVP coach? When I put this question to the business leaders, HR executives, and coaches interviewed for this book, a set of common themes emerged from among diverse perspectives:

- Business experience
- Credibility
- A proven track record
- High-level experience
- Cultural sensitivity
- Credentials and training

Business Experience

Not surprisingly, real-world business experience ranks at the top of nearly everyone's list of the most sought-after characteristics in an MVP coach. Barbara Fuchs, Director of Talent Development at UBS Financial Services, speaks for many when she identifies the ideal coach as someone who has "chosen to go into coaching as a second career," has "fifteen to twenty years' experience" in the MVP's business sector, "has had his or her own challenges," and "really understands the challenges executives face." The capacity of a coach to empathize with the MVP – to understand exactly what the MVP is going through – is clearly of central importance for Fuchs. That capacity is directly tied to experience.

Denise Lockaby, Director of Professional Development at The Stride Rite Corporation, and Kevin Pennington, Senior Vice President and Chief Human Resource Officer at Rogers Communications, also emphasize the importance of extensive business experience. "I look for someone who has a broad business background," says Lockaby, while Pennington stresses, "At Rogers, we look for people who are seasoned business professionals." But Lockaby and Pennington assign a somewhat different value to experience than Fuchs does. Experience, they point out, enables coaches to help MVPs deal with a crucial determinant of their success – organizational dynamics. As Pennington puts it, "We want coaches who can understand organizational dynamics and who understand power and politics in the organization." So the coach should be someone, says Lockaby, "who has worked in large complex organizations."

Ed Piccolino and Paul Larson address the issue of experience from the coaches' perspective. Piccolino, formerly Vice President for HR at PepsiCo International and currently President of Piccolino Associates, LLC, and Vice Chairman of MHW Ltd. (a wine and spirits importing business), as well as an adjunct coach at Right Management, is often asked to coach MVPs, first of all because of his specific business experience: "I've been associated with places that have a strong brand of talent development, and that creates a positive halo in the minds of the potential person being coached. The second reason I think I get selected is that I have been a successful business person myself." Uniquely, Piccolino's business experience addresses both management and talent development. In turn, Paul Larson, also of Right Management, attributes his success in attracting coaching assignments involving MVPs to strong leadership experience: "I think we are often chosen to coach MVPs based on our experience. I have been a leader in an organization. I led two different businesses for Johnson and Johnson many years ago: one, a turnaround of a division in England for J&J and second, a company in California that J&J acquired. In the process I served on different boards for J&J and I now serve on other non-profit boards."

Credibility

To be effective, a coach must have credibility with his or her coachee. The issue is especially urgent for those who are coaching people as highly accomplished as MVPs. Clearly, a coach's business experience goes a long way toward establishing credibility. But the experience required in this instance is not so much general and wide-ranging as it is highly specialized. In fact, according to Vas Nair, Vice President and Chief Learning Officer at Schering-Plough, meeting this requirement is precisely what differentiates coaching MVPs from coaching other types of people: "Where I think coaching of top talent is different from other types of coaching is that it has to be a lot more targeted to the job that has to be done at the senior level. It could be, for example, about emotional intelligence, being more politically savvy, or about strategic skills. Coaching in these areas requires coaches who have had experience in specific competencies. The coaches who have personally 'lived' these competencies or experiences can help accelerate the colleague's learning and development."

The key point is that credibility goes to coaches "who have done it before" at the same level as the MVP. "We want someone," says Rogers Communications' Kevin Pennington, "who has a feel for or a direct experience in the function of the person they're coaching. Getting an accountant to coach a marketing guy probably isn't the right fit." Daniel Sonsino of Raytheon comments similarly: "We really like folks to have Fortune 500 corporate experience. If they also have defense or aeronautics or aerospace experience, this is even more of a plus." And Paul Larson offers a coach's point of view: "I think I get chosen because I've got the in-the-chair experience. I'm working with an individual now who is a VP and heir-apparent to running a multi-billion dollar division of a technology-based company. I was chosen to coach him partly based on my experience." In order to be credible, a coach must have specialized experience, as Paul Larson puts it: "in-the-chair experience."

Proven Track Record

It hardly needs saying that someone's previous *coaching* experience is as important to coaching an MVP as his or her *business* experience. A coach must have a proven coaching track record. Michal Lindemann says that only those coaches with whom the firm has had a long-standing relationship are trusted to coach its MVPs. "The coaches I use for the MVPs have to have a proven track record over time," says Michael Lindemann, "I'm only going to let coaches near my MVPs if I've known them for five years or more. They have to have handled a variety of assignments and situations. I have been able to throw something at them and they've been able to take it and run with it."

High-Level Experience

Whether the coach's track record includes experience helping MVPs get to the next level – which is often a high-powered leadership role – is a crucial factor to consider during the selection process. As a coach, says Karen Steadman, President of Leadership Futures, "you have to make sure that you have a very solid value proposition for why your coaching of MVPs can be helpful both to the individual and to the organization. MVPs are already successful. They have probably already got a lot of publicity and already know they're successful. They need to be coached by someone who knows what got them there and what it will take to get them to the next level. So the value proposition I present as a coach is, 'You're great now, but I can help you to get to the next level.'"

For Bill Roiter, Managing Partner of MVP Research, helping MVPs reach the next level often means helping them meet the new challenges associated with senior leadership: "These MVPs may be put in a role because they have a proven track record and are brought in to drive change in the organization and to create a performance-driven organization. To drive this change, they need to learn organizational political savvy and to influence and get a point across. The higher up they go, the more they need to develop the skill to influence people and bring them on board and get them aligned around their vision. In their previous role, they may not have had that skill but they were still able to drive towards results. It's almost a different set of skills that is required to take them to the next level." Roiter adds that he is often brought in to coach an MVP precisely because he has experience helping MVPs acquire this high-level, leadership skill set.

Cultural Sensitivity

As discussed in Chapter 1, the organizations most in need of developing and retaining their MVPs are often globally active enterprises for whom the impending talent shortage may be most acute. Doing business on a global scale necessarily means fostering relationships with employees, as well as clients, from many different cultures. The ideal MVP coach needs the sensitivity to deal with cultural diversity. As Barbara Fuchs of UBS Financial Services notes, "Since we are a global organization, I need coaches who have the experience of working with MVPs from other cultures and countries. We have a number of executives who move to the U.S. from other parts of the world, particularly Switzerland. Sometimes we have cultural differences that turn into leadership challenges. We often use a coach to work with the executive on how to manage those cultural differences and be successful in their new role." Winnie Lanoix, a long-time executive coach with Right Management, confirms that she is selected because she has coached many "other" MVPs: "Many of the people I coach are people who are either international or working globally or managing a global virtual workforce." Lanoix herself grew up in Geneva, Switzerland, in an international family and spent time studying cultural transitions and competence, and therefore understands that the cultural nuances MVPs must master as a global understanding is often a prerequisite to senior-level positions in today's companies.

Credentials and Training

Coaching is a professional activity. External coaches, consequently, should have professional qualifications and credentials. A number of companies that I interviewed require that coaches be certified with such organizations as the International Coaching Federation (http://www.coachfederation.org).

Laurie Cowan, Director of Organizational Development at CSL Behring doesn't "worry about the degree that the coach holds." She does, however, "worry about coaching certification. The coaching certification helps coaches to be a little bit more results oriented." While Cowan prefers someone with "an organization development background over a psychology background," Scotiabank's Naomi Shaw reveals that the bank prefers its coaches to be organizational psychologists. But they too must be certified by the International Coaching Federation, or a similar body.

Some organizations see the coach's credentials as working hand in hand with the presentation of a professional process. Denise Lockaby, Director of Professional Development at The Stride Rite Corporation, says: "I look for somebody who's had training in coaching and who has a process and outcomes. When I interview a coach I ask them to describe their coaching process. What is the process, what is the outcome, what are the milestones along the way and how do you measure success?" She explains that the coach's process supports his or her credentials as evidence of professionalism. Such clearly defined processes are often provided for coaches who work with consulting firms.

Creating a Coaching Pool

Large, sophisticated organizations normally have coaching needs that no one or two external coaches could possibly meet. Closely related to the task of choosing a coach, consequently, is creating a pool of coaches that the organization can draw from as needed. Two key considerations motivate organizations when creating such pools:

- Only coaches the organization intends to develop a long-term relationship with should be chosen for the pool.
- Coaches should be chosen to create a pool that is both functionally and culturally diverse.

Preferably the coaches should share the same coaching philosophy and methodology.

For organizations where globalization is important it is preferable that the coaches are tied into a common reporting system in order to know who is being coached where and to ensure consistent evaluation and feedback. For instance Right Management has a Coaching Management System (CMS) which supports leader and executive coaching initiatives in organizations by providing online tools that measure progress and impact. CMS demonstrates the value organizations receive from their investment in coaching. For clients with multiple coaching assignments that cross geographic or business unit boundaries, Right's CMS offers a means to work with multiple coaches while managing standards of services and evaluation processes.

Let's examine these two considerations in more detail.

Form Long-Term Relationships

Many organizations find coaches they trust and then stick with them. At the Chubb Group of Insurance Companies, reports Vice-President of Leadership Development Eileen Mathews, "We tend to have relatively longstanding relationships with different suppliers of coaching services, including individual proprietors and companies that have a cadre of coaches they supply. So over time, I think they've really come to know us."

As Mathews implies, a prime advantage to the company of forming long-term relationships with coaches is that the coaches become familiar with the culture and goals of the organization. Bob Hedley, Corporate Vice President of Leadership and Human Resource Management Systems at Maple Leaf Foods, makes the point more directly: "Over the years we've developed good relationships with a few specific people. It's really important for anybody working with Maple Leaf that they understand what it is we're trying to accomplish, that they understand our values and what we're trying to get at." Debi King, Senior Vice President of Human Resources at MDS Inc, comments similarly: "We want people who fit the value and the culture. We're selecting people who the HR teams knows and who have had success in the organization before, or we're selecting people who the line executives and general managers have either used before or who they know and who they're comfortable with." The emphasis is on the organization knowing the coaches and the coaches knowing the organization.

Build Functional and Cultural Diversity into Your Pool

I noted above that the ideal coach is sensitive to cultural diversity within an organization. I could add that the ideal coach also offers a diverse range of functional competencies. Since many coaches are excellent but rarely ideal, organizations meet multifarious needs by building diversity into the coaching pool. Says Meg Jones, Senior Vice President for Human Resources and Chief Learning Officer at The Children's Hospital of Philadelphia: "We try to build a very broad group of coaches with a lot of different skill sets; so we pay a lot of attention to diversity in terms of our coaches." Where Jones pinpoints skills, Michael Lindemann highlights cultural diversity: "You have to have a really diverse group of coaches because diversity is increasingly important at senior levels. To be credible you have to have a group of coaches that mirrors the diversity of the organization."

For Lindemann, interestingly, the object of a diverse coaching pool is not always to match coaches with coachees of similar cultural backgrounds. In fact, he sees value in matching people from very different backgrounds: "You may also want to provide a coach who brings a fresh perspective. For instance, if the person to be coached is a white guy from America, then give him a coach from Japan who has a very Japanese perspective on the world."

In the end, the goal of building diversity into the coaching pool is similar to the goal of establishing long-term relationships with coaches: organizations seek coaches who can understand them. For this reason, Shell, as its Vice President of Resourcing and Development Mike Conway says, uses "a few organizations with robust standards and a global reach rather than lots of ad hoc coaches. The providers are identified by our Learning function and they work with them to ensure alignment and a shared point of view."

Orienting Coach to Company

Many companies take proactive measures to ensure that their pool of external coaches acclimatizes to the ways and mores of the organization. They enlist coaches in a formal orientation process. In most instances, senior leaders brief coaches on the organization's culture and values, as well as on the issues facing the company and the industry. Their next step is to explain the company's talent management process and address how coaching fits into the leadership development process. The coach often receives an in-depth session on the organization's assessment approaches and tools.

Keith Lawrence, Director of Human Resources, provides a succinct account of orientation efforts at Procter & Gamble: "We've done training with the pool of coaches that we have selected. We make sure that they understand the current business priorities – what's happening in the organization – to make sure that they are fully up to speed to help them coach the P&G folks appropriately."

At the time of writing, I am assisting a large international organization to recruit a cadre of coaches to work with 900 high-potential leaders. The company's year-long leadership development program calls for contributions from a number of different coaches at different stages of the process. To ensure that the many coaches understand the program's objectives, they will gather from around the world to attend a one-day orientation session in Europe. Here, coaches will learn about the company's background, culture, and brand, along with its strategy and values. They will also be given an overview of all the elements of the leadership development program and the role of coaching in each element. A clear account of the results that they are expected to deliver will also be provided. The session will be delivered, in part, by members of the company's Global Executive Team and senior executives.

Orientation sessions at some organizations are even more extensive. At PepsiCo International, for example, the orientation process lasts for four-and-a-half days. Brian Chitester, PepsiCo's Vice President of Organization Development and People Capability, describes how the program unfolded for coaches at one such event.

> They needed to learn how to coach against the criteria that we wanted them to use. They needed to be able to integrate feedback from Lominger, Hogan, and our 360 process and

integrate the managers' input. They had to be able to do it in a way that was effective within our culture. So we introduced them to the Lominger and Hogan tools and encouraged them to get the full certification. We then put them through two simulations where they actually had to put a coaching and development plan together based on these case studies and get feedback on that plan. Then they had to do a second one. That gave us pretty good insight into the people who attended the program, and we knew which ones we were going to use for which assignments and which ones we wanted to use for our more senior and high-potential people.

Orientation at PepsiCo clearly has a double purpose: not only to acquaint coaches with "what it's like to coach in this culture" but also to evaluate a coach's strengths in order to deploy him or her most effectively within the organization.

PepsiCo's program, Chitester further explains, involved contributions from long-time PepsiCo coaches and from the CEO himself: "Some long-term coaches, like Dr. Marty Seldman, who's coached at PepsiCo for 25 years, came to talk about their experiences and what they were like. Our CEO also came in to talk about what he's trying to do in changing this culture, in getting people ready for these big roles and what he needed from these coaches. He also spoke about his own coaching experience in the past."

An example of a typical agenda for a coaching orientation session is provided below.

Sample Agenda for Coaching Orientation

Agenda
8:00 a.m. – 2:30 p.m. Room TBD
2:30 – 3:00 p.m. Company Tour
3:00 – 5:00 p.m. Site Visit

Continental Breakfast	7:45 – 8:00
Welcome and Introductions	8:00 – 8:15
Opening Remarks	8:15 – 8:30
• Company History, Vision, and Values • Company Growth • Human Capital Strategy • Q & A	8:30 – 9:15
• Company Strategic Vision and Growth • Departments and Cross-Functional Relationships • Organization Structure • Current & Future Challenges • Q & A	9:15 – 10:45
Break	10:45 –11:00
Strategic Coaching Program: • History, Current State, Future State • Review Guidelines • Review Roles and Responsibilities and Coaching Process Flow • Metrics • Q & A	11:00 – 12:00
Catered Lunch	12:00 – 12:15
Talent Management: • Talent Management Web site and online development resources • Performance & Development Plan • Leadership Performance Survey • Competency Models • Q & A	12:15 – 1:15
Round Table Discussion: • Coaching Best Practices • What has worked at the company and what has not?	1:15 – 2:30
Tour of a Facility • Challenges facing organization	(2:30 – 3:00 Travel) 3:00 – 5:00

Matching Coach and Coachee

Once coaches have been selected for the coaching pool and have been oriented to the company, the next step in organizing coaching for the MVP is to match a coach with a coachee. Once again, organizations tend to be very deliberate in their approach to this matching process.

Teri Kozikowski, Vice President of Global Organization, Staffing and Development at GE Real Estate, provides a good indication of the considerations to take into account when making the match: "Number one has got to be chemistry with the person who is being coached. It's just as important to know who the person is who is being coached as it is to know the coach. We want to match up the personality, match up the experiences, match up the age if that makes a difference, and match up the gender if that matters. Language obviously is important. So it's really making sure that you've got two people who are going to be able to respect each other and connect."

Debi King of MDS Nordion also stresses the importance of making a careful selection based on chemistry: "We spend a lot of time matching the appropriate coach with the individual. We really believe that there's an art to the matching of coach and coachee, that chemistry is essential for that, as well as the specific experiences and focal areas of the coaches. They really need to match up with the style and expectations of the coachee."

In addition to chemistry, GE's Kozikowski addresses a consideration that applies to MVPs in particular: "I would add that MVPs are hungry for coaching from somebody whom they respect. You've got to pair them up with somebody who has had the business experience and the coaching experience. That person must be able to draw on examples of people the coach has worked with before and demonstrate the successes. MVPs are not going to respect somebody who says, 'Oh, I think this might work.'" As we see, a point made earlier re-emerges: MVPs must be coached by people who engender their respect. An MVP coach must have credibility.

Daniel Sonsino of Raytheon speaks of making a match on the basis of "style" rather than "chemistry": "When we choose coaches we look at their style. For instance, if a person has to improve their communication style because they're too brash or they don't speak out enough and share their opinion, we'll find a coach who exhibits those characteristics personally because when they exhibit that characteristic themselves they can help develop it in other people. So we spend a lot of time on matching the right person to coach our MVPs." The personality of the coach, then, is another important consideration.

Shell's Mike Conway prefers to focus on specific needs for key staff when making a match. Says Conway: "Coaching is primarily done by line managers and HR staff. External coaching is used very selectively and pays off when it addresses a well-articulated need that both the company and the employee can see. Once these needs have been clearly defined, we can then determine who is the best coach to work with a specific individual." Scotiabank's Naomi Shaw similarly addresses skills: "We've categorized the coaches according to the required skills. So if somebody needs assistance in developing strategy, we have a cadre of coaches to address that issue. If it's regarding presentation skills or communication, we have another cadre of coaches. When somebody comes to us with a request, we find out what the need is and then we provide them with a list of three different coaches they can select from."

As Shaw makes clear, coachees often play a central role in making a match. At UBS Financial Services, people requesting coaching are provided with three profiles: "Then it's the responsibility of the coachee to set up the screening interview with the coaches whose profiles look interesting to them," explains Barbara Fuchs. "If they don't find someone who is a good fit for them among these three people, they can come back to us and ask for additional profiles." The practice at LoJack, as Mark Bornemann, Vice President of Human Resources and Risk, describes it, involves giving "the coachee the opportunity to interview two to three coaches. We want someone who is going to really mesh with them. If you force a coach on somebody, they may resent it. The more they don't mesh, the less they want to share and open up. So we get someone who has a similar background."

Paul Barrett, Vice President of International Operations at LoJack, recounts his experience of having conducted such interviews: "I interviewed three different coaches. With two of them the chemistry wasn't right. The third was a person who had been a CFO of a company. He was a little bit of an older gentleman, seemed very measured, very calm, and wanted to listen. The other two people were talking at me, as opposed to listening. This third person took some time to listen to me and so I made the decision to go with him. I thought that the chemistry was better than with the other two. I was happy with my choice."

Coaches themselves can sometimes take part in determining which is the most appropriate match for them. As Arabelle Fedora, the Southern region coaching leader for Right Management explains:

> We spend a long time asking questions of the HR business partner and sometimes of the individual's boss. This allows us to match the potential coachee with the right coach. We have to get a good sense of what might be important in terms of credibility. For instance, an MVP who is dealing with multiple strategic business issues may need a coach with experience in a similar corporate environment. In other cases the MVP may need a coach who is skilled at helping build a team. In all cases, we ask many questions in order to recommend coaches who will be the best match.

The Coaching Process – What to Expect

The final step in organizing coaching for the MVP is to get on with the coaching itself. But what can the organization reasonably expect the actual coaching process to look like? Right Management, a well-known and successful coaching organization, follows an eight-stage process that normally lasts six months but can be as short as three months or as long as twelve. Right's process is, obviously, specific to Right, but most coaches and coaching organizations follow steps that are similar to the following. Note that the coachee is called a "leader" in the outline below.

1. Enrolling the Individual Client

The selected coach meets with the leader to be coached and his or her manager to ensure that all are clear about the coaching objectives and expected outcomes. The enrollment step concludes with a "confidentiality agreement" outlining what information may be shared outside of the coaching relationship and with whom.

2. Building the Relationship

The coach and leader meet to get to know one another, exchange information, and map out the coaching process and activities. The relationship builds over time, focusing on what is most critical to the well-being and growth of the leader and the organization.

3. Fact-Finding and Feedback

A range of assessment tools are used to develop a complete picture of how the leader's style, personality, and behavior are related to on-the-job effectiveness. (The various assessments and tools have been described in Chapter 3.) Confidential interviews are often conducted with the leader's manager, colleagues, and direct reports to gather "real world" feedback and insight. This information is used to diagnose development needs, providing a foundation for a professional development action plan.

4. Development Planning

The coach works with the leader to ensure the quality and viability of the development plan. Specifically, the coach reviews the plan to make sure that:

- It is focused. Priorities are clear and kept to a manageable number.
- It is specific. It outlines specific behaviors that will be changed or improved.
- It is realistic. Goals are achievable and actions are feasible.
- It addresses needs in a variety of ways. A number of strategies are employed.
- Success is measurable. The plan includes clear, measurable criteria and timeframes.
- Resources are identified. The leader knows where to go for help.

The development plan is then shared with the manager, and all parties agree on how progress will be monitored.

5. Coaching to the Development Plan

This phase of work involves coaching to the plan and to real-time issues. The coach will help the leader become aware of specific issues that others have identified as areas to improve upon, and will come up with specific development plans that are timely and achievable. Coaching may involve skill building, role playing, preparing for key events, and debriefing relevant real-life experiences. Having had the opportunity to practice and apply what has been learned between sessions, the leader will have the chance to discuss experiences with the coach and to get additional help on how to be most effective in his or her role.

6. Monitoring Progress

The coach works with the leader to ensure that the goals of the plan are being achieved, that learning is ongoing, and that new issues are being dealt with effectively. Depending on the agreement, the coach may provide periodic progress reports to the leader's superior and/or the sponsor of the coaching engagement.

7. Closure/Evaluation of Success

Since the objectives of each coaching effort are different, success looks different in each case. After the completion of each coaching assignment, the coach meets with the individual and his or her boss to review the objectives and assess how well those objectives were met. In addition, the coach may conduct follow-up interviews with the leader's boss, colleagues, and direct reports, and look at other comparative data in the form of climate surveys, customer feedback, and other relevant performance criteria.

8. Planning Next Steps

Maintaining a view toward the future ensures that the leader is clear about next steps as he or she continues to implement the development plan and ongoing execution of behavioral change.

Checklist for Organizing External Coaching for MVPs

❑ Choose a coach with
- Business experience
- Credibility
- A proven track record
- High-level experience
- Cultural sensitivity
- Credentials and training.

❑ Create a coaching pool and
- Form long-term relationships
- Build diversity into your pool (both culturally and functionally)

❑ Orient coach to company by organizing a well-planned orientation session.

❑ Match coach to coachee, taking into consideration chemistry, personality, needs, skills, and experience.

❑ Ensure that coaching proceeds according to a well-defined process.

CHAPTER 8

The Role of HR in Coaching and Talent Development

The contributions of HR (an organization's Human Resources department) to the coaching and development of MVPs have received intermittent attention in several of the previous chapters. This chapter will examine HR's role directly. In particular, I will address how HR contributes to the identification of MVPs and how it ensures that such identification is consistent and fair. I will then move on to discuss HR's role in creating development opportunities, before giving extensive treatment to its role in developing an overall approach to coaching. The chapter will conclude with a brief consideration of how HR can provide coaching directly. The roles we will discuss, then, for HR are as follows:

- Identifying talent
- Ensuring consistency and fairness
- Supporting development
- Supporting coaching

Identifying Talent

HR's role in identifying talent goes beyond assisting with individual selections. It consists, most importantly, of creating a comprehensive talent management process. "My role," says Vas Nair, Vice President and Chief Learning Officer at Schering-Plough, "is to help establish what I would refer to as the *foundation* when it comes to people development – our learning and development strategy." While the talent management process is overseen by the CEO and line leaders, HR plans this process and assists with its implementation. In Nair's words, "the process supports the foundation. To more effectively execute the talent management activities, we provide specialized training for the HR team and line leaders."

Keith Lawrence, Director of Human Resources of Procter & Gamble Beauty and Healthcare Products, spells out the "several things" that HR does throughout the company: "A very rigorous system is used to identify the 'Next Generation Leaders.' It is owned by line management and facilitated by HR. We invest significant time in detailed reviews of candidates, looking at their performance in building both the business and the organization. Rich discussions from multiple points of view ensure we are making the right decision – for both the individual and the company."

At CSL Behring HR is, according to Laurie Cowan, Director of Organizational Development, accountable "for the talent review and succession planning process." She adds that HR is also "accountable for building the capabilities of the HR generalist staff to support their client group. We believe that the talent is owned by the organization and that it is senior management that needs to create the development opportunities. We are building the capabilities of senior executives to own the process." If talent is "owned by the organization," instead of by any particular group or team, then it is HR's job to work with senior management to ensure that MVPs are identified and developed in the interests of the larger organization.

Shell's Vice President of Resourcing and Development, Mike Conway, adds that in global businesses HR can deliver "tremendous benefit" by "aligning selection processes, simplifying them and making them absolutely standard worldwide." Shell identifies high-potential staff by means of a technology known as Current Estimated Potential (CEP – see Chapter 3 for more details about CEP). "HR," says Conway, "has a key role to play, first of all in that we own the technology. Secondly, we set the agenda and the timetable for the business. HR in the business has a key role to play in being expert facilitators on the ground. They roll out and manage the process in the business and ensure that it is run to standard and on time. They are quite simply our leaders in the field."

Ensuring Consistency and Fairness

Applying the talent identification process with consistency is essential to identifying talent fairly and ensuring that the organization's pool of MVPs reflects the diversity of its overall employee and customer base. For large global organizations that are active in diverse markets, consistency and the fairness and diversity that derive from it have particular import. They are absolutely essential to attracting and retaining the talent necessary to support global expansion. As noted in Chapter 1, managing talent effectively is a crucial organizational function in a world facing an impending talent shortage.

It cannot be taken for granted that consistency and fairness are applied in talent identification. As we saw in Chapter 2, research conducted at Shell revealed that women and staff in Asia may have lower indicated potential than the rest of the staff and the process for assessing them may be less reliable. Similarly, technical staff tended to have lower indicated potential than commercial staff. Left unaddressed, this situation at Shell may simply have continued. It was Shell's HR function that identified the issues and has taken the lead in addressing them.

As the Shell example demonstrates, consistency and fairness often require intervention. And HR is normally in the best position to lead the pursuit and in many organizations this is precisely what it does. For example, Michael Lindemann lists overseeing workplace diversity among his many responsibilities. Wendy Watson, Executive Vice President of Global Services, describes the role of HR at State Street Corporation: "Because our CEO has some pretty aggressive goals on diversity, HR has helped in the identification of where talent and diverse people are in the organization. They prompt the managers to look more closely as to whether that person should be on the emerging talent list. They ensure that we look across the organization at women, people of color, and non-U.S. passport holders and that we identify who we should move into that top talent pool. We need to be more aggressive than we have been in the past."

Ellen Moore, President of Chubb Canada, provides the perspective of senior management: "I think HR needs to play the role of traffic cop. They need to present equal opportunities for a lot of our high-potentials. They need to make sure that we're reaching deep enough and broadly enough across the organization. They need to make sure that senior managers are not biased in favor of their own staff. Their job is to make sure that we're presenting equally from all business units and all geographies, and that we're not missing any opportunity." She succinctly sums up HR's role in applying consistency and fairness across the board: "They're the employee advocate."

Supporting Development

Identifying MVPs and high-potentials is not an end in itself. If selection isn't followed by a well-structured program to accelerate their development, then selection itself is at risk of becoming pointless. Another crucial function of HR, therefore, is to ensure that such a program exists for MVPs – that meaningful development opportunities are created for them and that they, in fact, avail themselves of these opportunities.

Paul Mayer, head of U.S. Human Resources for the Altana group of companies, could be speaking of Human Resources departments in general when he describes his own role: "In essence, I am a clearinghouse or the central point of development for these high-potential individuals in the organization. I look at people who managers have brought to my attention and ask, 'How can we help develop and assist in their growth? Where can we send them for training? What type of educational processes should we create for these individuals? Where might they by a few years from now?'"

Eileen Mathews, Vice President Leadership Development at Chubb, describes HR's role similarly: "They make sure that all the pieces are in place, that all the players are enrolled, and that the employees get what they need. I see them as being a right hand to the manager in terms of talking through options with the manager or the employee and making sure that we craft the best possible experience for the employee. The HR groups in the different locations really are our distribution arm. They make sure that people get shepherded to the right place at the right time."

"Shepherding" would also be a good description of HR's role at State Street, as would "sounding board." Says the company's Executive Vice President of Global Services, Wendy Watson, of her HR department: "They drive the review program and provide quarterly updates to the senior leadership team. More importantly, they provide help in sourcing internal candidates. If you've got a top-talent individual, they are able to help you see where there's a good match in terms of a job opportunity. They also act as a sounding board, helping you think about how to develop a person or giving advice if you're trying to deal with a difficult problem with one of these folks."

Supporting Coaching

One particular way HR supports MVP development is to play a leading role in designing, implementing, and managing the organization's coaching programs. In Chapter 7, I provided detailed descriptions of the steps organizations take to establish an effective external coaching regime. Here I would like to address the specific contributions of HR to coaching regimes, both external and internal.

Designing a Program

HR typically initiates the creation of structured programs for the internal and external coaching of MVPs. To plan an effective program, HR must at the outset think through a number of central questions. These questions address:

- **The definition of coaching** – What is coaching? When should coaching be used? Who is eligible for coaching?
- **Strategic fit** – How does coaching as a leadership development tool fit the organization's larger strategy and business objectives?
- **The coaching process** – What will coaching actually involve? What will happen, why, and how? How do we make sure the process is transparent?
- **Selection** – How is a coach to be selected? Who establishes the criteria? How are the specific engagement needs determined and communicated?
- **Orientation** – How will the coach be familiarized with the company? What critical organizational and engagement-specific information needs to be provided, and who will provide it? (For the typical elements of a coaching orientation program, see Chapter 7.)
- **Confidentiality** – What proper boundaries should the coach observe between keeping information confidential and disclosing it to the organization? The question is particularly

important for the coachee, who must be assured that legitimately confidential information will remain confidential.

- **Performance metrics** – How will success be measured and monitored, both in-process and at the conclusion? Who will be involved? (This topic will be covered more fully in Chapter 10.)

Addressing these questions is a necessary prerequisite for the formulation of a sensible coaching program plan. Once they have been answered, implementation can proceed.

Implementing the Program

The following steps are involved in implementing the program.

Selling the Program

In many cases, the first step in implementing the program plan involves selling it. As discussed in Chapter 2, MVP development of any kind is unlikely to succeed without the active support of senior management. If that support doesn't already exist, HR's first task is to acquire leadership buy-in. Leadership must be convinced to take a hands-on interest in the initiative.

Once senior management is on board, HR must turn its attention to selling the program among MVPs and high-potential employees. This second task in the selling process is no less crucial than the first. Since coaching, as we have seen, was once primarily considered a remedial "fix-it" activity, HR must ensure that MVPs and others have a proper understanding of the wide-ranging purposes and benefits of coaching. It should do so by providing MVPs with a clear overviw of how coaching supports leadership development within the context of the organization's business strategy and business objectives.

Creating the Coaching Pool

A second major task in implementing a program plan involves selecting actual coaches and organizing them into a pool. We looked at selection and pooling in Chapter 7. Here I will confine myself to a few additional comments that pertain specifically to the role of HR.

Creating a coaching pool is normally HR's responsibility. How, then, does HR typically go about identifying coaches who have the potential to join the pool? When HR at PepsiCo International set about creating a coaching pool, the company sought input from both internal sources and external partners, in this case assessment firms. "The first thing we did," explains PepsiCo International's Brian Chitester, "was to touch base with all our field HR people and ask them who they were using as coaches. We talked to Lominger and Hogan – two of the assessment firms that we use – and asked them what coaches they use around the globe. That way we began to build a pool of coaches." In similar circumstances, MDS Nordion's HR department relied on internal sources, canvassing individual HR people but also line executives and general managers, according to the company's Senior Vice President of Human Resources, Debi King. Daniel Sonsino reports that HR at Raytheon approached partners such as coaching firm Right Management for suggestions.

Screening the Coach

HR must not only identify candidates for the coaching pool but must also screen them and make final selections. Chapter 7 contains a comprehensive list of qualities that should be taken into account when choosing a coach. The following questions are of particular use for HR in determining two of those qualities, a candidate's track record and qualifications. These questions are designed for HR to put to external coaches, but they may readily be modified for selection of internal candidates.

What to Ask the External Coach

1. Tell me a little bit about your coaching qualifications and the type of services that you provide as a coach.
2. Since the establishment of trust is so important to a coaching relationship, specifically what do you do in order to establish trust with a new client?

What to look for in a response:
  * Appreciates the importance of trust
  * Has a sense of what he or she needs to do to build a safe relationship
  * Recognizes the need to establish a relationship with all stakeholders and knows how to proceed.
3. Describe to me one of your most successful coaching engagements.
What to look for in a response:
  * How was success measured?
  * Who did what to make it succeed?
  * Was credit shared?
4. Tell me about a time when you had a very challenging coaching assignment. What did you find most difficult about the assignment? What happened at the conclusion of the engagement?
What to look for in a response:
  * Shared responsibility (cause and cure)
  * How was the client's anger dealt with?
  * How did the coach handle the pressure?
5. Describe what you would consider to be an unsuccessful coaching engagement. What did you learn from it? What would you do differently?
6. Describe the process you follow when you have a new client. What are the steps from the beginning to the middle and the end of the coaching engagement?
What to look for in a response:
  * Is there a clear process?
  * Is there flexibility in the process?

Defining Roles and Responsibilities

Once HR has selected coaches and established a coaching pool, its final task in implementing the organization's coaching program is to define the roles and responsibilities of coachee, manager, coach, and HR itself. Clarifying these roles and responsibilities at the outset prevents misunderstandings and confusions that can doom the coaching engagement to failure before it even begins.

Chris Keller, now the Director of Talent Development at McGraw Hill, describes how other companies where he has worked handled role definition: "We had a standardized process in terms of expectations around what we wanted the individual to prepare before going into an assignment so that he or she could articulate to a coach his or her needs and interests. Prior to that, we standardized an approach that the manager of the individual used to take part in the assignment and work with the individual to identify some of those developmental interests. We prepared a template for the HR person who was co-ordinating this. And then we determined expectations for the coach around what he or she would need to follow in terms of clarifying an assignment, briefing after the first one or two meetings with the coachee and with the coachee's manager."

An example of how HR might define roles and responsibilities follows.

Coachee

The coachee works with the coach as a collaborative partner in the coaching program. The coachee must be open to being coached – willing and able, that is, to participate in a value-added process that will help him or her continue to grow and be successful in the organization. To succeed, coachees must

- Be serious about their intent to change
- Be involved in helping finalize the selection of coach
- Be ready to work and to receive feedback
- Be willing and able to keep commitments, to be open with the coach, and to participate fully in the program
- Create and/or revise their development plan, and be willing to try new ways of learning

Sponsoring Manager

Managers must support coachees throughout the coaching engagement. The support they provide may include:

- Helping the coachee finalize selection of his or her coach
- Ensuring the coachee is aware of his or her development needs through open and honest feedback and through participation in 360-degree surveys or interviews, if requested

- Meeting with the coach and coachee early in the process to review coaching objectives
- Reviewing the development plan with the coach and coachee and discussing the support and/or resources the manager will provide
- Providing feedback to the coachee throughout the coaching program
- Meeting with the coach and coachee near the end of the coaching program to review outcomes

Coach

As a professional advisor, the coach will guide the coachee through a personalized development process designed to meet predetermined coaching objectives and business goals. During this process, the coach will:

- Inform himself or herself about the coachee's role and background within the company
- Work with the coachee and sponsoring manager to set clear coaching objectives and create a development plan linked to business objectives
- Meet regularly with the coachee to discuss progress on the development plan
- Focus on problem solving and provide honest and direct feedback
- Support the coachee in setting up feedback systems and support structures
- Use real-time events to help the coachee learn and develop
- Review progress with the coachee and sponsoring manager at certain points in time

Human Resources

HR can make a number of contributions to coaching activities beyond simply engaging the coach. These contributions may include:

- Preparing the sponsoring manager for his or her role in the coaching process
- Preparing the coachee – informing him or her of exactly what is involved and what he or she has to do at each step of the process

- Arranging for all coaches concurrently involved in coaching assignments within the organization to meet and discuss common themes that may be emerging from individual engagements
- Communicating any such themes, particularly as they relate to organizational and business issues, to senior management

Managing the Program

Once in place, the coaching program must be managed. This too is a key HR function. As Brian Chitester of PepsiCo International explains, HR's practical hands-on contribution typically involves choosing candidates to be coached (usually in co-operation with sponsoring managers), matching the candidate with an appropriate coach, and then monitoring the coaching engagement as it proceeds: "My basic role is to put together the process against which we, one, select people for coaching and then, two, identify coaches and match them with coachees. And then, with the help of HR I manage the process while the coaching is happening to ensure that we're fairly consistent in our approach and that we're integrated against all the other PepsiCo processes and tools that we use so that the coaching results in pretty integrated feedback." Teri Kozikowski, Vice President of Global Organization, Staffing and Development, for GE Real Estate, adds that monitoring also involves evaluating progress: "I get reports back from the coaches in general around how things are going. If something's not going well, I hear about that. I don't want to know about the specific details of the conversation. That's confidential between the coach and the employee. Our concern is to make sure we are seeing the results in the area that we targeted. And also, quite frankly, making sure that the person who was assigned a coach is following through."

Of all the interviewees who spoke about the role of HR in managing specific coaching engagements, Barbara Fuchs, Director of Talent Development at UBS Financial Services, provided the most detailed account. Her comments are worth quoting in full:

> Someone from talent development meets with line managers before the process starts. If they haven't used executive coaching before, we'll explain to them what executive coaching is, the process, what will happen if they and the person to be coached

decide to go forward with the coaching. And then we let them know that they will be pulled in and asked to contribute in this person's development.

We send the HR business partners a report on a monthly basis on what's progressing as far as the coaching relationship goes. The coach should also reach out to the HR managers if there are any issues that come up – the coach should keep them informed of what's happening. They will also be called in if they're going to have a meeting with the line manager, and the coachee will also have the HR partner come in and sit in on the meeting.

And then we manage the process. We do spend a lot of time on the front end in terms of driving the expectations of what's going to happen in the coaching engagement. If coachees are going to spend six months doing something for their personal development, we want to make sure they're doing what's aligned to the competency model, their 360 results, their performance and development and what their manager wants them to develop. So we spend a lot of time on the front end defining the expectations and the goals of the coaching engagement. Then we'll do a mid-point check and then a final wrap-up that addresses the goals that they started with in the first place – were they able to achieve them? We'll have their manager actually assess changes in behaviors or changes in performance based on the original goals.

Coaching

Some HR departments not only supervise and otherwise support coaching but provide coaching itself. In order to be effective coaches themselves, HR professionals are often given formal training. At MDS Inc., for example, as Jim Reid explains, the top 20 or so professionals have been "put through the leader coach program, which is a disciplined way to help people who are business partners to line managers to be more effective at performance coaching."

Training is also provided for HR professionals at GE Real Estate, reports Teri Kozikowski. Such training consists of role playing exercises examining the differences among coaching, mentoring, and serving as an HR business partner. "GE," says Kozikowski, "does a really nice job of helping HR professionals understand their role as a coach. You can't be a good business person without also being able to coach. So, good coaching involves an understanding of the business itself and an understanding of the person and how to help him or her optimize his or her own actions. We wanted to reinforce that understanding in the Real Estate HR community. So we developed a half-day seminar for our global HR team. It reinforced the role of a coach versus mentor, and helped HR Managers overcome some of the tougher things that you might encounter when you're supporting a senior leader who really needs some coaching."

This chapter has examined the role of HR in the coaching of MVPs. What has emerged from our discussion is a picture of HR as the organization's central authority for overseeing the MVP's development, especially by means of coaching. Almost nothing of importance to the coaching and development of MVPs happens without the involvement of HR. But, as we will see in the next chapter, the manager has a significant role to play as well.

Summary of HR Roles in Coaching and Talent Development

- Identifying talent

- Ensuring fairness and consistency

- Supporting development

- Supporting coaching

  - * Designing a program
    - o Defining coaching
    - o Considering strategic fit
    - o Planning the coaching process
    - o Planning selection
    - o Designing an orientation program
    - o Creating a confidentiality policy
    - o Designing performance metrics

  - * Implementing the program
    - o Selling it
      - – Providing an overview of coaching's purposes
      - – Getting leadership buy-in, if necessary
    - o Creating a coaching pool
    - o Screening coaches
    - o Defining roles and responsibilities

* Managing the program
  - o Matching coach and coachee
  - o Ensuring alignment between coaching goals and business goals
  - o Monitoring progress
- Coaching

CHAPTER 9

The Role of the Manager in Talent Development and Coaching

Most development of talent takes place on the job; as we noted in Chapter 4, on-the-job experience can account for up to 70 percent of an MVP's development. MVPs' jobs are therefore ideally structured to ensure that MVPs learn and develop new skills, or their learning takes place naturally on their existing job. Remember, one of the key characteristics of MVPs is that they *want* to learn and grow. They are also highly marketable and are sought after by recruiters and other companies. If they do not feel they are developing in their existing job, they will either find another job in the organization or will look for a job in an organization that *will* help them develop. However, if MVPs are developing and progressing in the way they would like to, they are unlikely to seek a job elsewhere or take calls from other companies and recruiters. Managers are the ones who are in a position to ensure that MVPs continue to learn and grow in their existing job. Managers therefore play a critical role in on-the-job development of talent – and in retaining that talent in the company. Managers need to remember that MVPs are highly self-motivated and that whether or not they give their MVPs coaching and support, these individuals *will* develop. Not that this lets managers off the hook. On the contrary, it is in their best interest to keep their MVPs challenged and happy so that they stay on the team and so that the team, and ultimately the company, performs well. A key mantra is: "People join a company but leave a manager."

In this chapter we will take a closer look at the manager's role in developing MVPs and high-potentials, including the overall importance of the manager in talent development, the specific role of the manager as coach, the differences between the manager's role as coach and the same manager's everyday role, the training that is provided for managers to be coaches, and the manager's role in the engagement of an external coach. We will also talk about situations in which managers are not capable of coaching MVPs, and solutions to this problem.

Role of Manager as Developer of Talent

Development of talent is a key component of a manager's job. In fact, in my interviews, two company presidents (the ultimate managers) emphasized talent development as a key part of their jobs. "Particularly in an organization such as this one that is rapidly growing and evolving, the development of high-potential people is critical to my job," says Canada Pension Plan Investment Board President David Denison. Chubb Canada President Ellen Moore states bluntly, "Development is probably my number one job." Moore adds that she sees herself as being like the coach of a sports team: "You've got to be able to assess the roles and make sure that people are rising to their level of performance and that the team can ultimately perform at its highest level."

Eileen Mathews, VP of Leadership Development at Chubb aptly describes the manager as a "gatekeeper" whose role is to ensure that the MVPs and high-potentials obtain the level of development that is most appropriate for them. "The managers help the MVPs to assess where their big challenges are and help them to obtain the right kind of experience to help overcome these challenges," says Mathews. She explains that these experiences might include participating in an internal general development program, an external general development program, or a special assignment or project. She further adds that after the appropriate development experience has been implemented, it is then the manager's role to "help keep the balance between the business side of the MVP's development and what the MVP is learning from these development experiences."

MDS Inc.'s Executive VP of Global Human Resources, Jim Reid, echoes Mathews' perception of the manager as gatekeeper in his description of the manager as the one who creates the path to greater development for the MVP. "We have to make sure we are giving MVPs challenging and big jobs. We have to make sure that we've cut a path out for them and that they are being rewarded financially. We have to make sure they're working with people they respect and from whom they can learn."

Ideally, one of the key people MVPs can learn from – especially MVPs at the junior or middle levels – is the manager. (For MVPs at more senior levels, external coaching is often more appropriate; we will discuss the manager's role in the engagement of an external coach later in this chapter.) Some managers balk at the suggestion that they have to take on the role of coach. They may feel that it takes too much time away from doing their "real job." They don't realize that there are times when it is entirely appropriate for them to take on a coaching role. This is because, as the MVP's manager, they are well positioned to identify the specific areas in which an MVP needs developing and to provide guidance on improving those areas. Once a specific area has been identified, such as, for example, setting strategy at a high level, the manager can say to the MVP, "I'm going to act as your coach in helping you develop your abilities in the area of setting strategy."

The benefits of coaching are not just one-sided – that is, on the MVP's side. There can be definite rewards for managers, too. State Street Corporation's Executive VP of Global Services, Wendy Watson, is adamant on this point. "Developing people can be fun," says Watson, "especially if it's a more junior person who is at an earlier stage of their career. You can visibly see them develop over a very short period of time. It is very rewarding to see somebody who has not had that much business experience develop and grow so fast. At this stage of their career they can be like a sponge – they are so anxious and willing to do well. They want to learn, they want to get ahead, and so that aspect of the mentoring or coaching is really fun."

But, as much fun as it can be, there is no question that "coaching" is separate and distinct, in both purpose and approach, from "managing." Below, we will look at the differences between the manager's roles as coach and as manager.

Differences Between Manager's Role as Coach and Everyday Role

During the usual course of their job, managers are expected to lead teams of people to achieve the required business results and objectives. This means setting out clear team and individual expectations, making sure that the appropriate actions take place, and monitoring effectiveness. All too often, the manager's interaction with his or her direct reports involves holding brief or ad hoc meetings with teams and individuals and communicating via e-mail or conference calls. Coaching, on the other hand, requires that the coach and MVP set aside specific and dedicated time to focus, together, on the development of specific skills and competencies that the MVP requires in order to do their current job better or to build competencies that will enable them to progress in the organization. It's not too difficult to see that the two functions require very different approaches. The following chart puts the differences into sharp relief:

Managing	Coaching
Competes	Collaborates
Directs/Tells	Develops/Listens
Reinforces hierarchy	Reinforces networking
Holds back information	Shares information
Encourages dependency	Encourages self-management
Dictates	Solves collaboratively
Allows less autonomy	Allows more autonomy

Training Managers to be Coaches

Recognizing the central role managers play in coaching, and also recognizing the very different approaches a manager must take to "coaching" versus "managing," organizations are making special efforts to provide managers with appropriate training. Such training usually consists of workshops. At Scotiabank, reports Naomi Shaw, Vice President, Leadership, "we provide a one-day coaching workshop for our vice-president level and above. The bulk of the session is really about putting coaching into practice. Participants partner up and one person puts the coaching tactics into practice. The other partner hears details about the situation and then acts as the coachee in the role play. The coachee gives the coach feedback and then they switch places." At Schering-Plough the Situational Coaching Workshop lasts for two days. Vas Nair, Vice President and Chief Learning Officer, points out that the workshop "is a cross functional forum which focuses on such questions as: 'What is coaching when you're a line manager? What is coaching when you don't have direct reports but you influence others – for example, on a project team?' We provide managers with skills, tools and guidelines, together with a list of development suggestions, to use with their staff. The workshop provides participants with a non-threatening environment to practice their coaching skills."

Rather than an off-the-shelf training course, Schering-Plough's workshop is carefully designed to address its managers' specific coaching needs: "What is valuable about the two-day situational coaching workshop is that we built it from the ground up," says Nair. "We went out to our HR community and line leaders and said, 'Tell us about the coaching challenges you're faced with.' We got that input and we designed the case studies and role plays to target those needs. The feedback we've received is that the workshop material is very 'real'. Participants learn a great deal from the role plays and case studies as they are similar to the scenarios they are challenged with on the job. The cross functional set-up further encourages the 'coaching' discussions, as the solutions are viewed from different perspectives."

At Maple Leaf Foods, coaching training for managers takes place at different levels and through different programs. According to Bob Hedley, Corporate Vice President, Leadership and Human Resource Management Systems, the company offers both basic and advanced coaching skills training. The company also includes a coaching training component in its Performance Appraisal and Development Plan program. As Hedley explains, "We train managers on how to work with their employees to create a developmental action plan and how to do performance coaching versus career coaching." Yet another Maple Leaf Foods coaching skills program, Leaders Coaching Leaders, is run in conjunction with the external master coaches at the Niagara Institute. This program addresses issues such as how to initiate conversations or how to negotiate boundaries: "For instance if I'm the vice president and I'm coaching a young director," Hedley explains, "where is the boundary between when I should say, 'No, that's something you should take back to your manager and talk about' and when I should say, 'These are grounds for us to have a conversation'?"

Elements of a Training Program

Training programs for managers typically consist of the following elements:

- **Assessments:** Managers go through the same kinds of assessments that their employees go through and receive the same type of feedback. (See Chapter 3 for the types of assessments that they may experience.) By going through these assessments, managers have the experience of receiving feedback in a variety of areas and gain awareness of the assistance that a coach can give in debriefing the assessment feedback.
- **Creation of development plan:** Creating their own plan helps the manager to work with their employees to create a development plan.
- **Learning about team and organizational dynamics:** Being aware of these kinds of dynamics better equips managers to coach their own MVPs to develop skills and navigate their way around the organization.
- **Contracting to be a coach:** Managers learn how to create a contract with the MVP they are going to coach. The contract specifies what issue(s) will be covered in the coaching sessions.
- **Learning the various elements of the coaching process.**
- **Learning the boundaries of coaching:** Managers learn when to coach and when to refer people to other resources.
- **Learning when to end the coaching process and go back to normal business.**

I recently had the experience of coaching managers on how to be coaches. These managers worked for a global financial services company that was having difficulty retaining its top talent. The managers really wanted to develop their MVPs and other employees but did not have the process and tools to do this. I worked with the head of HR to create a one-day program that gave the managers all the tools they needed to identify development learning needs, to create a development plan, and to help them select the most appropriate approach to develop specific skills and competencies. During the seminar the managers also engaged in a series of role plays designed to give them the experience of going through the various stages of the coaching process. Clearly the program set up the foundation for coaching. In order to sustain and further develop the coaching approach, the company's HR division continued to support the managers in coaching their employees. The end result was that the retention rate of MVPs and many other employees increased dramatically.

What Managers Do as Coaches

Once the manager has received the necessary training, he or she can sit down with the MVP or high-potential to discuss coaching. It is important for both the manager and the MVP to realize and remember that during the coaching session, they are going to be interacting in a way that is quite different from their usual manager/employee role. Manager and MVP will need to contract with each other to set aside an hour or two every week (or whatever length of time is desired) to work on the specific issues that have been identified as being in need of developing. During the time that has been specifically set aside as coaching, the manager needs to remind the employee to view them as someone they can turn to as an advisor and teacher, as well as a day-to-day manager during the normal course of their work.

What kinds of things does the manager do in the role of coach? To answer this question, I sat down with a former colleague of mine at Fidelity Investments, Kathy McGirr. (McGirr, now retired, was the Senior VP of Talent Management at Fidelity at the time when I was the VP of Human Resources of one of the business units.) Together, we reflected on our experiences as managers, as well as our experiences coaching managers on how to develop their MVPs. Here is what we concluded that successful managers do during the coaching process. (Note that in compiling this list, we also considered the experiences of people we knew who were *not* successful coaches!)

As a coaching manager . . .

- Be clear about the competencies the MVP requires for success, especially those that they require in order to move on to the next level or job. Remember that, as coach, you can facilitate a change in behavior but you can't change a person's DNA structure or essential nature.
- Set clear expectations, and make sure the MVP is aware of these expectations.

- Provide detailed performance feedback honestly and respectfully.
- Make observations on areas where the MVP is doing well, as well as areas where they might improve or do things differently.
- Provide positive reinforcement.
- Refrain from telling the MVP what to do. Instead, guide the individual through the development and learning process; for example, by asking questions about how they might solve a problem and then providing your own insights.
- Provide perspectives on the company, strategy, direction, and so on, that will help the MVP take a broader view of the organization.
- Help the MVP to get back on track, as required.
- Outline the consequences of any actions the MVP might take or be considering taking.
- If the relationship is not working, salvage it and improve it, or help the MVP to leave the organization gracefully.
- If your lack of knowledge or skill prevents you from assisting the MVP, help them find internal or external resources that can assist. Let them know where they can look for help.
- Know when it is appropriate to bring in outside resources (such as external coaches).

In one professional services company I am familiar with the managers were very effective coaches for their extremely talented employees who were soon to be managers themselves. The managers would typically spend between one and two hours every two weeks in coaching their employees. They were completely committed to doing this in order to develop the skills and competencies of their staff. They would spend time teaching the individuals new skills and would also suggest internal and external training courses that would be helpful for these individuals. These coaching meetings were very different from the normal meetings held with staff. The latter meetings typically focused on client projects, business development, and organizational issues – rarely were they focused on people development. The result of this coaching approach was that the managers really helped to build a solid cadre of middle managers in the firm, who in turn would be able to develop their own employees.

The Manager's Role in the External Coaching Process

As we have discussed previously, it is sometimes appropriate to bring in an external coach for an MVP. This is especially true in cases where the person in need of coaching is at a senior level. However, as Brian Chitester of PepsiCo importantly points out, "The executive coach is not a surrogate for the role of local manager as talent developer." That said, there are times when, as Chubb Canada President Ellen Moore explains, the manager has to step back as coach because they are intricately involved in setting the performance expectations and compensation levels for MVPs. "At that point in time," says Moore, "the MVPs may not be coming to me in an advisor role. Therefore I have to establish an environment in which there are safe places for them to go. This means that they can go to each other for support, or sometimes I need to bring in external coaches or mentors for them."

Bringing in an external coach does not mean, however, that the manager steps right out of the process. In most successful external coaching engagements, the manager plays an integral role at each stage of the engagement. The engagement process is outlined in Chapter 7. Here we will look in more detail at the role of the manager at each stage of the process.

Identifying the Coaching Need

It is usually the manager who identifies the need for an MVP to have external coaching. This need is often identified in the context of performance and talent management discussions with HR or an HR consultant. In these discussions, the manager plays a key role not only in deciding that external coaching is the best method for developing the MVP but also in determining the objectives and results to be sought from the coaching engagement. It is worth remembering that the coaching need must be tied both to business goals and to the development of competencies in the MVP.

Matching Executives and Coaches

Typically, the manager asks the HR function to source potential coaches to work with the MVP. (See Chapter 7 for a discussion of creating a pool of coaches and Chapter 8 for the role of HR in the coaching process.) In some cases, it is the MVP who is to be coached that decides on the appropriate coach. In other cases, the manager has a say in determining the appropriate coach; choosing this latter arrangement further enhances the partnership between the MVP, the coach, and the manager. (A fuller discussion of matching coach and coachee can be found in Chapter 7.)

Creating Coaching Goals and a Development Plan

The manager initially meets with the coach to have what Meg Jones, Senior VP for Human Resources and Chief Learning Officer at The Children's Hospital of Philadelphia, calls a "really frank discussion" about the areas in need of development, and to provide feedback before the coach conducts the initial assessment of the MVP. In some organizations, there is also an initial meeting of the manager and coach that *includes* the coachee to talk through the goals of coaching in order to make sure everyone is on the same page. At these initial meetings, the manager defines the issues and needs and the results he or she expects to see from the engagement. The manager also plays a key role in framing the contract between the coach and the MVP. The contract spells out specific and measurable targets.

Michael Lindemann stresses that the involvement of the manager in external coaching is "utterly crucial." "If you don't do this well, then you're wasting your time and efforts and money." He explains that in his experience, preparation for the coaching enagement includes a "very lengthy preparatory interview" with the manager and the coachee individually, and that the results of each assessment are shared with the other (with the permission of each). "The coach would then facilitate a three-way meeting to come up with a development plan."

Monitoring Progress

After the initial assessment, feedback, and contract-setting session, the manager steps aside, and the coaching proceeds in a confidential manner between the coach and the MVP. However, the manager does have an important part to play in assessing the success of the coaching engagement through regular performance-monitoring updates at pre-defined intervals throughout the coaching process. By doing regular assessments, the manager ensures that targets are being met and, in a larger sense, the company mitigates the risk of the coaching assignment failing or going off the rails.

In addition to monitoring, the manager may also be asked by the coach to assist with specific learning activities that the two have determined are required to develop the MVP's competencies. The level of the manager's involvement in the coaching process itself is entirely up to the company.

Assessing Outcomes and Effectiveness

After the coaching engagement is complete, the MVP, the coach, and the manager sit down again together to review the progress made and the effectiveness of the coaching engagement in relation to the targets specified in the coaching contract. At this point, the manager also provides feedback on any behavioral changes that have occurred (or not occurred), based both on his or her own observations and on feedback from others. In some cases, as at The Children's Hospital of Philadelphia, the final meeting also includes the MVP sharing with the manager what he or she needs from the manager in order to be successful in the days and months after coaching.

What Happens When the Manager is Not Capable of being a Coach?

In an ideal world, all managers are not only keen on coaching their most valuable performers but are capable and effective in providing that coaching. In reality, there are a whole variety of reasons why a manager may not be capable of providing effective coaching. These run the gamut from managers who do not have the necessary coaching skills (despite training) to MVPs who, because of their own advanced knowledge and/or skill level, do not have anything to learn from a particular manager. Recently I had a conversation with an MVP who sought my advice. He had been identified as a high-potential and had gone through the company's program for high-potentials. The company president had then asked him to consider moving to a two-year assignment in an operational role. This was going to be a great opportunity for him to round out his existing competencies. However, he was concerned that he had nothing to learn from the manager of the operational unit. Our conversation focused on his need to identify other people in the organization who could help him develop during his assignment, or to ask if he could be provided with an external coach. (Clearly, the new manager would have to be in agreement with this latter request.)

There are also personal reasons why managers may be incapable of coaching. In some cases a manager may be jealous or resentful of an MVP who is on their team. Instead of recognizing that they can help the individual to achieve their goals, the manager does everything they can to put the individual down or to encourage them to leave.

In all of these cases, it is the responsibility of HR or the manager's manager to ensure that the MVP is either moved out of his or her current job or is given the appropriate support in the organization (or both). It is not just losing an individual employee that is at stake, but losing a lynchpin in the organization. As Wendy Watson says, "I'm currently mentoring a couple of people who are working for me and helping them become stronger, and this is good for my business and for the whole company." In other words, managers need to realize the importance of setting aside their own personal feelings for the greater good of the organization. In doing so, they will likely find that, ultimately, it comes back to reflect well on them.

Summary of the Manager's Role in Coaching and Talent Development

- Managers have a significant role to play in either providing coaching directly or supporting an external coaching engagement for MVPs

- In their role as coach, managers:
    * Identify the talent that can benefit from coaching
    * Receive training on being a successful coach
    * Learn to distinguish between their coaching role and their manager's role
    * Set aside specific time with their MVP to provide coaching
    * Help the coachee to view them as a coach, not a manager, during coaching sessions

- For external coaching engagements, managers provide the following support:
    * Identify a need for coaching
    * Assist HR in matching coach and coachee
    * Create coaching goals and development plan
    * Monitor progress
    * Assess outcome and effectiveness

- Managers must be prepared to set aside any personal feelings to help the MVP achieve their goals

CHAPTER 10

Coaching Benefits and the Return on Investment

Coaching is not an inexpensive undertaking. It can, in fact, be perceived as a costly proposition, in terms of both the money spent and the time involved. Some companies view the cost of providing coaching and other leadership development activities as a waste of money or as an unnecessary use of resources. Fortunately, this is not the case with the companies I interviewed. They recognize that company growth is dependent on the development of key talent. However, these companies, and others, do want to know why they are undertaking coaching initiatives and how they will know whether or not these initiatives are successful. In short, they want to see tangible evidence of the return on their investment. Increasingly, therefore, coaches and management are being asked to demonstrate both the benefits derived and the return on investment (ROI) from coaching. Is coaching worth the investment? Is it making a tangible difference in employee performance and – ultimately – the bottom line?

Demonstrating the benefits of coaching, especially the financial benefits, is not as straightforward as demonstrating the return on investment from, say, a specific change in a production process. It can be difficult to prove that a change in an employee's performance or behavior, such as improved leadership skills, was the direct cause of an increase in sales. As Nancy Lockwood points out in "The Challenge of Determining the Return on Investment of Executive Coaching," "There is . . . no standard set of metrics yet established to determine the ROI of executive coaching. Further, the nature of executive coaching is that results are both qualitative and quantitative – thus the story of executive coaching does not easily reduce to a single percentage when dealing with human beings."[1]

This does not mean that it is impossible to demonstrate the benefits of coaching. It does mean that HR and management need to be specific and clear about the goals – the key deliverables – that they want to achieve from coaching initiatives. The benefits of these initiatives can be determined only if the process and the desired outcomes from coaching are clearly identified and articulated. "You have to be clear about what you are trying to get out of each engagement, and you have to have experienced and qualified coaches to achieve the required goals and objectives," says Barbara Amone of UBS Investment Bank. Maple Leaf's Bob Hedley echoes this opinion: "If you're going to make the investment . . . you have to have a clear set of expectations and goals and shared responsibility from the company and the individual."

The identification of clear and specific goals is a process that organizations of all kinds, not just for-profit businesses, are undertaking these days. And in an era of increased accountability, organizations are also recognizing that they need specific tools for measuring whether their goals are being met. Without specific, measurable, achievable targets in place, it is unlikely that organizations will achieve their goals. When it comes to achieving coaching goals, as Mark Bornemann of LoJack points out, "there has to be a clear contract up front with the coach, together with a documented process, progress reports, and assistance with pre- and post-assessment of behavior change." Thus, the setting of development goals must be accompanied by the establishment of metrics for assessing whether those goals have been accomplished. Bob Levenson puts it this way: "The question is what are we trying to do with our talent management process in a larger sense? What are we trying to accomplish and what are the metrics?"

The company representatives I interviewed listed various goals (benefits) they sought to accomplish from coaching initiatives, and they described the ways they assessed whether or not those benefits were being achieved. In this chapter, we will look at both the benefits and the metrics used for measuring them. As for determining ROI in financial terms, mathematical methods do exist for measuring the impact of a training program on bottom-line company performance;[2]

1 Nancy R. Lockwood, "The Challenge of Determining the Return on Investment of Executive Coaching," January 2005. *Executive Coaching Series, Part 1*. Society for Human Resource Management. www.shrm.org/research.
2 See, for instance, the White Paper by Paul Bernthal, "Methods of Calculating ROI and Bottom-line Impact," Development Dimensions International, Inc., 2004.

however, the organizations I interviewed tended to focus more on the qualitative than the quantitative benefits of coaching. We will take a closer look at what they had to say about ROI later in the chapter.

The Benefits of Coaching

My conversations with company CEOs and other representatives elicited many benefits that companies look for from coaching initiatives. Among the key ones I heard enumerated are that the coachee:

- Is ready for the next promotion
- Develops better skills and behaviors
- Gains different perspectives and insights
- Becomes a good role model for others in the organization
- Becomes a more adaptable leader

Ready for the Next Promotion

For companies that are developing their talent so they can take on senior positions in the firm, readying an individual for the next promotion is the most obvious benefit of coaching. Canada's MDS Nordion and Maple Leaf Foods are among the companies that use coaching for this purpose. "We think that coaching gives people the opportunity to be groomed and to become great candidates for an executive position," says Nordion's Debi King, while Bob Hedley of Maple Leaf Foods observes, "Our satisfaction comes when we can say this person is ready for the next major challenge."

Develop Better Skills and Behaviors

At Raytheon, coaching is used because, as Daniel Sonsino explains, the company has "seen explicit changes in our leaders' behavior in going through the leadership and coaching programs. People have elected to select coaching as a developmental program because they've seen their leaders change or improve or develop."

Gain Different Perspectives

Procter & Gamble's Director of HR, Keith Lawrence, believes that "the benefit [of coaching] to the individual is that they are gaining additional insights that will accelerate their growth and development."

Good Role Model for Company

Naomi Shaw, Brian Chitester, and Vas Nair all see the value of coaching in creating good role models for their respective companies. Shaw sees the role model as someone who can become a spokesperson for why ongoing coaching and development are important at Scotiabank, while Chitester calls PepsiCo's coachees "developmental zealots," who have experienced the process and can, in turn, themselves become good coaches for the company. Vas Nair explains the importance of the role model in terms of improving employee morale at Schering-Plough: "After completing the Situational Coaching workshop, we have a group of people who become champions of our cause. They become the next generation that's going to take up the concept of coaching and development and seek out opportunities to further enhance performance management and talent development. This sends a strong message that Schering-Plough is very serious about its people and people development. It helps us sustain a culture of high performance which has a positive impact on morale."

Adaptable Leaders

The accelerating rate of change in the national and global business economies has spurred many companies to build capacity for change into their processes so that they can continually reinvent themselves. Leadership development and coaching initiatives can help both organizations and individuals to develop this capacity for change. "The reality," says Shaw, "is that we don't know what's going to happen. We try to ensure that we have a very adaptable leadership so that we will be better prepared for the unknown."

For Scotiabank and other companies, coaching provides what Shaw calls a "cadre of people who are more flexible and adaptable. This adaptability comes," she explains, "because we focus on experience-based learning and on moving people from one business line to another or one functional area to another."

The broader experience that coaching provides can be especially beneficial for the individual who has worked for the same organization for most of his or her working life. Michael Lindemann stresses the importance of the external coach in bringing the larger perspective (and thus greater adaptability) to such a person. "The external coach by definition is someone who is maybe working with two or three very big companies in a single day," says Michael Lindemann, "so they can really talk about the bigger picture, and this can be tremendously refreshing for a person who has spent a long time in the company."

Other Benefits of Coaching

In addition to the benefits the companies I interviewed cited, there are other documented benefits of coaching. These include behavioral changes, such as enhanced self-awareness of the implications of typical behaviors, improved influencing skills, deeper understanding of how to coach others, ability to empower greater collaboration between departments, and improved ability to deal with interpersonal conflicts.[3]

Assessing the Benefits: The Difficulties of Calculating Financial ROI

Many times organizations will ask if it is possible to calculate the return on investment from coaching. As mentioned above, mathematical methods do exist for calculating the impact of training programs on the bottom line. The companies I interviewed, however, stressed the difficulty of relating the effects of coaching directly to increases in profitability. One difficulty they pointed to is the number of variables involved. One of my own coaching experiences provides a good illustration of this difficulty. I was asked to coach the president of a business unit of a large and successful firm. The individual had recently been promoted into the position and was struggling with making the shift from being a tactical manager to being a president who had a clear vision that was understood by all. Our coaching engagement

---

3 Lockwood, January 2005.

focused on creating a strategy and getting all the key stakeholders to buy into it.

By the time we had completed the coaching engagement, the president's business unit had the largest gross and net revenue of all the business units – amounting to many millions of dollars. At the same time, the level of employee satisfaction in the business unit had increased by about 10 percent, due in part to the fact that the employees now all had a clear sense of where the business was going and the part they played. It would be great to say that my coaching had a significant impact on the business and that the ROI was very impressive. But how could I prove that it was my coaching that had caused this change? The individual was very motivated to learn, and once he had the data and the tools to succeed, he took his business unit to the next level. At the same time, the business environment for this particular business improved, and this improvement could well have played a major role in the successful outcome.

Another difficulty in proving ROI is pointed out by representatives of companies that are analytical in nature and thus require rigorous proof of the numbers. Jim Reid of MDS Inc. echoes this sentiment. "We are a science-based company, and 'show me the data' is one of the favorite expressions among our employees."

Raytheon's Daniel Sonsino points out that for his engineering firm "the difficult part of calculating ROI is that everybody is going to look at every minute detail. If you say you can get 100 percent return on our investment for coaching, that just opens the way for a number of engineers and analytic types to determine if you're right or not. We don't really want people spending their time doing that."

So in the face of these difficulties in determining ROI from a financial perspective, how *do* companies demonstrate the benefits of coaching?

Assessing the Benefits: Measuring Success Indirectly

From my interviews, I discovered five metrics companies use to track the benefits of coaching:

- Rate of retention
- Promotion rate

- Engagement (commitment to the company)
- 360-degree feedback surveys
- Anecdotal evidence and observations

These metrics could be called "indirect" measures of success; for instance, a company is certain its coaching is working because the retention rate of its MVPs has increased, but it can't *directly* prove that coaching is the reason for the increase.

Retention

For many companies retention is just one of several measures of the success of coaching; however, for other companies, the rate of retention of employees is the *key* metric. There are good reasons for this. MVPs and people with high potential are by definition very marketable. They are well-known, not only within their own organizations, but often externally as well. This means, of course, that they are often sought out by other organizations, and therefore retaining them becomes a priority for the organization. As Right Management adjunct Executive Coach Ed Piccolino notes, "Organizations that build a strong external and internal brand as a place that develops talent are able to retain talent and are less susceptible to talent poaching. This gives them a competitive advantage in the marketplace."

A number of the people I interviewed believe that coaching and leadership development play a significant part in the retention of MVPs in their respective companies. Companies that cite retention as a "key metric" include Millipore Corporation, The Stride Rite Corporation, MDS Inc., and Maple Leaf Foods. In fact, at Maple Leaf Foods, retention of key people is the "only" metric used to determine return on investment from coaching.

As mentioned above, science-based MDS Inc. is one company that doesn't believe it is possible to have a good financial measure for ROI from coaching. "However," says Jim Reid, "we are very good at knowing who our MVPs are and tracking their retention. So our metric is primarily retention of top talent." The same is true for Rogers Communications. "We do not have a financial measure," explains Senior Vice President Kevin Pennington. "We believe that if a person feels wanted and that we have developed them, we will retain them and they will perform better."

Promotion Rate

Readiness for promotion is another one of the key benefits of coaching that we discussed in the Benefits section above. An obvious metric for determining this benefit, therefore, is the *rate* at which MVPs and high-potentials are promoted after they have gone through various leadership development and coaching programs. "I can tell you," says GE Real Estate's Teri Kozikowski, "that of the people we have assigned coaches to over the last three years, all have improved in the particular area we wanted developed, and most have been promoted."

Chitester calls the rate of promotion at PepsiCo the "proof of the pudding" (of the benefits of coaching) and has the statistics to back it up: "About 70 percent of the people who have been through the leadership development and coaching process in the last two years are being promoted to bigger and broader positions."

Engagement

It stands to reason that companies that invest in their employees through talent development and coaching – that is, that show their employees they matter – build higher levels of engagement and commitment in those employees. Employee engagement is measured by scores on employee engagement surveys. Maple Leaf Foods and Pepsi-Co are two companies that use such surveys – what PepsiCo terms "organization health surveys" – as a metric for determining the benefits of coaching. "The results of these surveys," says PepsiCo's Chitester, "show that people who have been through our leadership development and coaching process are dramatically higher – 20 percentage points higher – on all of the key indicators compared with their peers who have not been through this process."

360-Degree Feedback Surveys

Raytheon is one company that measures the benefits of its talent development process not from the perspective of return on investment but from the perspective of what its Senior Manager of Talent Management and Succession Planning calls "intrinsic value." To assess this intrinsic value, the company relies on its 360-degree feedback ratings.

"We do a 360 on the front end of the coaching engagement and then repeat it at the back end," explains Daniel Sonsino. "We're looking to find out things such as: Did the person benefit from the coaching? Did their manager find value in it? Did they see a change in their behavior? That's where we really focus our ROI."

Anecdotal Evidence and Observations

Closely related to using surveys as a metric for tracking the benefits of coaching is relying on observations and anecdotal evidence. In fact, much of the data concerning the benefits and positive outcomes from coaching come from such anecdotal evidence, gleaned from managers, coaches, peers, and even the coachee.

At Chubb, as Eileen Mathews explains, anecdotal and direct observation center on the following types of questions: Are we seeing new behaviors? Are we seeing people engaging at a different level? Are we seeing different results? "A lot of times, managers of people who have been in coaching situations, or the HR clients I've been working with, will stop me in the hall and give me updates," says Mathews. "They're very quick to let me know about specific incidents where they see improved results. They'll say things like, 'I've got to tell you about Dan. I don't know what's going on, but in the last couple of months it's been very apparent that a big change has taken place in him.'"

Anecdotal evidence and observations may seem like a haphazard way to track success, but "anecdotal" doesn't have to mean "informal." At LoJack, for example, there is a formal process in place to track observations. "We have quarterly status updates with the functional head or the coachee's manager, myself, and the coach, and we will get together and review the action plan and where we are at," explains Human Resources VP Mark Bornemann. He adds that at the start of the coaching engagement, the coach will do personal interviews with the individuals and their peers and manager and then will repeat this process six months later, after the coaching engagement is finished. The coaches will ask those being interviewed if they have noticed a positive change in the coachee. "That's our ROI," says Bornemann.

Chubb Canada President Ellen Moore believes that the observations of the coachees themselves are the most important measure of success. Says Moore: "I think the key measure is asking the individual who is being coached how he or she feels about his or her job today versus six months ago. It's also about having that individual articulate a very demonstrable difference and whether he or she personally feels there's been a benefit. Of course," she adds, " this has to be validated by the observations of others."

Questioning the Question

Some would argue that there is no need to prove ROI to senior management. Among those who see no need to answer the question of ROI posed by senior leaders is Mike Conway, VP of Resourcing and Development at Shell International. "Anyone who has worked at senior levels and has been around a large organization for a while knows that coaching can be a very powerful instrument," Conway maintains. "The issue isn't whether coaching is a good thing, but rather what is the right way to provide it."

Conway also points out another crucial thing to keep in mind about coaching: you can't guarantee that it is always going to work. A native of Scotland, Conway uses the example of his country's national sport to make his point. "You can try to find a golf professional who will guarantee to cut your handicap by ten shots. But the golf pro can only do so much and the result may not be what you want. It may well be that through coaching you discover that there are indeed some things that the individual is either not very good at or more significantly just not prepared to take on."

I would add that this does not have to be seen as a *limitation* of coaching but can be an equally important "benefit" – that is, coaching can be a valuable tool not only for improving an individual's performance but also for finding out where their limitations lie. In "failing" to help a person to improve, you may be saving the company countless dollars in investing in an individual who is just not right for the job.

In an era of increased accountability, there is certainly a strong argument to be made for the importance of demonstrating the benefits of coaching. But Conway puts the whole ROI question into what some might see as a more realistic context: "My sense is that where you have a performance or capability gap and agree that coaching is part of the solution, then I think the way you ensure a return on investment is making sure you spend the money wisely with coaches who provide what you need."

The same could be said for developing talent in general. And "the very best outcome" is exactly what companies are looking for in developing their Most Valuable Performers.

Checklist for Demonstrating Benefits of Coaching

❑ You can demonstrate the benefits of coaching only if the process and desired outcomes of coaching are clearly identified and articulated. Among the key benefits of coaching are that the coachee:
* is ready for the next promotion
* develops better skills and behaviors
* gains different perspectives and insights
* becomes a good role model for others in the organization
* becomes a more adaptable leader

❑ Along with clearly identified goals and outcomes, you need to have achievable targets and metrics for determining the return on investment.

❑ Demonstrating ROI in financial terms can be difficult. Often it is better to focus on indirect methods of tracking success. These include:
* Rate of retention
* Promotion rate
* Engagement (commitment to the company)
* 360-degree feedback surveys
* Anecdotal evidence and observations

Participating Companies and People Interviewed

Alpha Trading Systems

Ian Hendry
Chief Administrative Officer

Prior to this position Ian was head of HR for Capital Markets, Royal Bank of Canada.

Altana

Paul Mayer
Human Resources

The name ALTANA represents a global specialty chemical group. It comprises the holding company ALTANA AG and four operating divisions: BYK Additives & Instruments, ECKART Effect Pigments, ELANTAS Electrical Insulation, and ACTEGA Coatings & Sealants. Altana currently has 31 production facilities and 45 application and research laboratories worldwide.

The group of companies with global operations has its headquarters in the German town of Wesel on the Lower Rhine. Foreign business accounts for 83 percent of its total turnover. The four divisions within the ALTANA Group all occupy a leading position in their target markets with respect to quality, product solution expertise, innovation, and service. Products made by companies in the ALTANA Group are sold in over 100 countries worldwide and their quality has earned the company an outstanding reputation amongst its customers as a valuable partner, both nationally and internationally.

Canada Pension Plan Investment Board

David Denison
President and CEO

The CPP Investment Board is managed independently of the Canada Pension Plan by experienced investment professionals to help sustain the future pensions of 16 million Canadians. The Board's role is to invest the CPP fund to maximize returns without undue risk of loss.

The Children's Hospital of Philadelphia

Meg Jones
SVP, HR and Chief Learning Officer

Since its start in 1855 as the nation's first hospital devoted exclusively to caring for children, The Children's Hospital of Philadelphia has been the birthplace for many dramatic firsts in pediatric medicine. The hospital has fostered medical discoveries and innovations that have improved pediatric health care and saved countless children's lives.

Today, The Children's Hospital of Philadelphia is one of the leading pediatric hospitals and research facilities in the world. The hospital's 150 years of innovation and service to its patients, their families and the community reflects an ongoing commitment to exceptional patient care, training new generations of pediatric health care providers, and pioneering significant research initiatives.

Chubb Insurance

Ellen Moore
President, Chubb Insurance Company of Canada
Eileen Mathews
Vice President, Leadership Development, Chubb Group of
Insurance Companies

The member insurers of the Chubb Group of Insurance Companies form a multi-billion dollar organization. For 125 years, Chubb has been delivering property and casualty insurance products and services for personal and commercial customers worldwide through 8,500 independent agents and brokers. Today, Chubb is the 11th largest property and casualty insurer in the U.S. and has a worldwide network of some 120 offices in 29 countries staffed by more than 10,000 employees. Chubb's global network includes branches and affiliates in North America, Europe, Latin America, Asia, and Australia. Chubb offers businesses more than 90 property and casualty and 80 executive protection and professional liability insurance products. In addition, Chubb offers an array of property and casualty insurance products for individuals and families with fine homes and possessions.

CSL Behring

Laurie Cowan
Director, Organizational Development

CSL Behring is a global leader in the plasma protein biotherapeutics industry. Passionate about improving the quality of patients' lives, CSL Behring manufactures and markets a range of safe and effective plasma-derived and recombinant products and related services. The company's therapies are used in the treatment of immune deficiency disorders, hemophilia, von Willebrand disease, other bleeding disorders, and inherited emphysema. Other products are used for the prevention of hemolytic diseases in the newborn, in cardiac surgery, organ transplantation, and in the treatment of burns. The company also operates one of the world's largest plasma collection networks, ZLB

Plasma. CSL Behring is a subsidiary of CSL Limited, a biopharmaceutical company with headquarters in Melbourne, Australia. For more information, visit www.cslbehring.com.

Fidelity Investments

Jennifer Harnden
Vice President, Leadership and Organization Development

Fidelity Investments is a group of privately held companies in the financial services industry. It is made up by two independent but closely cooperating companies, Fidelity Management and Research Corporation (FMR Co.), founded in 1946 and serving the North American market, and Fidelity International Limited (FIL), spun off in 1969 to provide investment products and services to clients outside the Americas. Fidelity Investments includes a large family of mutual funds, their distributors and investment advisors, and a retail brokerage, as well as unrelated businesses.

General Electric (GE)

Teri Kozikowski
EVP of Human Resources, GE Aviation Financial Services
At the time of writing the book Teri was VP, Global Organization, Staffing and Development at GE Real Estate.

General Electric Company (GE) is "Imagination at Work." From jet engines to power generation, financial services to water processing, and medical imaging to media content, GE people worldwide are dedicated to turning imaginative ideas into leading products and services that help solve some of the world's toughest problems.

GE Real Estate, a business unit of GE Commercial Finance, is a leading source of innovative real estate capital solutions. With a 28 percent compound annual growth rate since 1993, GE Real Estate is one of the fastest growing and most profitable real estate enterprises. Few institutions have the capital strength, industry knowledge, and global expertise to match GE.

Leadership Futures

Karen Steadman
President
Adjunct Coach with Right Management

Leadership Futures advises senior leaders and their organizations on sound investments in leadership talent. Services include executive assessments, accelerated leadership development programs, and performance optimization. For more information, visit www.leadership futures.com.

LoJack Corporation

Mark Bornemann
Vice President of Human Resources and Risk
Paul Barrett
Vice President of Operations

Today LoJack Corporation, the premier worldwide provider of wireless tracking and recovery systems for mobile assets, is the leader in global stolen vehicle recovery, with its unrivaled, proven solutions and direct integration with law enforcement. LoJack created the stolen vehicle recovery category over 20 years ago and has earned a more than 90 percent recovery success rate. Globally, more than 200,000 stolen vehicles worth over $4 billion have been recovered using LoJack technology.

LoJack operates in areas of the U.S. with the greatest population density, highest number of new vehicle sales, and greatest incidents of vehicle theft. LoJack is currently operable in 26 states and the District of Columbia, as well as in 29 countries throughout Europe, Africa, Asia, and the Western Hemisphere.

MDS Inc.

Jim Reid
EVP, Global Human Resources, MDS Inc.
Debi King
SVP Human Resources, MDS Nordion

MDS Inc. is a global life sciences company that provides market-leading products and services that are used by its customers for the development of drugs and diagnosis and treatment of disease.

Its three core businesses – MDS Analytical Technologies, MDS Nordion and MDS Pharma Services – are global industry leaders in the respective areas of life sciences tools, molecular imaging, and pharmaceutical contract research. These are robust markets that are expanding rapidly.

Along with well-respected brands and strong product and service capabilities, MDS offers strong company leadership. The management team is focused on increasing value for all stakeholders, and on doing business by the core values of trust, respect, integrity, and a commitment to excellence.

What makes it all work is attracting and retaining the right people – people who strive to deliver excellent results, and share our purpose of making a distinctive contribution to the health and well-being of people in our world.

Maple Leaf Foods

Robert Hedley
Corporate VP, Leadership and
Human Resource Management Systems

Maple Leaf Foods is Canada's leading food processor. Supported by its flagship consumer brands – *Maple Leaf®*, *Schneiders®* and *Dempster's®* – and a family of strong regional brands, they are market leaders across our businesses.

The Company's operations are organized into two major groups:

Protein Value Chain, includes value-added fresh and further processed meats and meals.

Bakery Products Group, comprises Maple Leaf's 88.0 percent ownership of Canada Bread, a leading producer of value-added nutritious fresh bakery products, frozen bread products, and fresh pasta and sauces.

Maple Leaf's goal is to build a globally admired meats and meals and bakery company, through meeting customer and consumers' needs for the highest quality, nutritious, and innovative food products.

Maple Leaf Foods has its headquarters in Toronto and employs 22,500 people at operations across Canada, the U.S., the U.K., and Asia.

The McGraw Hill Companies

Chris Keller
Director of Talent Development

Chris gave his perspective on coaching based on many years' experience in companies with robust coaching processes.

Merck & Co., Inc.

Michael Lindemann

Michael speaks about his experience of being directly involved in talent management and diversity at a number of well known global companies.

Millipore Corporation

Bob Levenson
Director, Global Talent Development

Millipore is a life science leader providing cutting-edge technologies, tools, and services for bioscience research and biopharmaceutical manufacturing. As a strategic partner, Millipore collaborates with customers to confront the world's challenging human health issues. From research to development to production, Millipore's scientific expertise and innovative solutions help customers tackle their most complex problems and achieve their goals. Millipore Corporation is an S&P 500 company with more than 6,100 employees in 47 countries worldwide.

MVP Research

Bill Roiter
Managing Partner

Bill Roiter, Ed.D., is a psychologist and businessperson with more than 25 years experience consulting to businesses. He is an executive coach in the Boston area. He was also the co-author of *Corporate MVPs* (Wiley, 2004) with Margaret Butteriss. His new book, *Beyond Work: How Accomplished People Retire Successfully* (Wiley, 2008), looks at how these valuable people move *beyond* *work* and set up their new lives. Bill can be reached at info@mvpresearch.com.

PepsiCo International

Brian Chitester
VP of Organization Development and People Capability

PepsiCo International (PI) peps up the world. A subsidiary of PepsiCo, the company makes and sells soft drinks, juices, fountain syrups, and concentrates under the Pepsi, 7UP, Mirinda, Mountain Dew, Gatorade, and Tropicana brands outside of North America. Most of its products are sold through franchised bottlers. Also included among PI's activities is the international sale of Frito-Lay and other salty-snack products. PepsiCo International has divisions in more than 200 countries worldwide; its largest operations are in Mexico (Gamesa and Sabritas snack brands) and the U.K. (Walkers snacks).

Procter & Gamble

Keith Lawrence
**Director of Human Resources, P&G Beauty and
Healthcare Products**

P&G is a recognized leader in the development, distribution, and marketing of superior fabric & home care, baby care, feminine care, family care, beauty care, health care, and snacks & coffee products.

P&G's growth has been dramatic. The company is now nearly twice the size it was at the beginning of the decade, generating more than $76 billion in sales last fiscal year. Other financial statistics are equally impressive.

Raytheon

Daniel Sonsino
Senior Manager, Talent Management and Succession Planning

Raytheon is a technology leader specializing in defense, homeland security, and other government markets throughout the world. With a history of innovation spanning more than 80 years, Raytheon provides state-of-the-art electronics, mission systems integration, and other capabilities in the areas of sensing; effects; command, control, communications and intelligence systems; as well as a broad range of mission support services.

Right Management

Stephen Doerflein
Organizational Consultant, Northeast U.S.

Arabelle Fedora
VP Organizational Consulting, The Southern Region Coaching Leader

Winnie Lanoix
Coaching Leader for the Mid-Atlantic U.S.

Paul Larson
SVP, Coaching Market Leader for Southern California

Dina Lichtman
SVP, Career Management Consulting, Northeast U.S.

Joy McGovern
Practice Leader, Attract and Assess, Northeast U.S.

Ed Piccolino
President of Piccolino Associates, LLC
Vice Chairman of MHW Ltd. – a wine and spirits importing business.
Adjunct Coach with Right Management

Rogers Communications Inc.

Kevin Pennington
SVP and Chief Human Resource Officer

Rogers Communications Inc. is a diversified Canadian communications and media company engaged in three primary lines of business. Rogers Wireless is Canada's largest wireless voice and data communications services provider and the country's only carrier operating on the world standard GSM technology platform. Rogers Cable and Telecom is Canada's largest cable television provider offering cable television, high-speed Internet access, residential telephony services, and video retailing, while its Rogers Business Solutions division is a national provider of voice communications services, data networking, and broadband Internet connectivity to small, medium, and large businesses. Rogers Media is Canada's premier collection of category-leading media assets with businesses in radio and television broadcasting, televised shopping, publishing, and sports entertainment.

Royal Dutch Shell International plc

Mike Conway
Vice President Resourcing and Development
Human Resources

Shell is a global group of energy and petrochemical companies, active in more than 130 countries and territories and employing 108,000 people worldwide.

Royal Dutch Shell is a global energy company. The company is active in more than 130 countries and territories and employs 108,000 people worldwide. The company believes that oil and gas will be integral to the global energy needs for economic development for many decades to come. Shell's role is to ensure that we extract and deliver them profitably and in environmentally and socially responsible ways.

Schering-Plough

Vas Nair
Vice President and Chief Learning Officer

Schering-Plough is an innovation-driven, science-centered global health care company. Through its own biopharmaceutical research and collaborations with partners, Schering-Plough creates therapies that help save and improve lives around the world. The company applies its research-and-development platform to human prescription and consumer products as well as to animal health products. In November 2007, Schering-Plough acquired Organon BioSciences, with its Organon human health and Intervet animal health businesses, marking a pivotal step in the company's ongoing transformation. Schering-Plough's vision is to "Earn Trust, Every Day" with the doctors, patients, customers, and other stakeholders served by its approximately 50,000 people around the world. The company is based in Kenilworth, N.J., and its Web site is www.schering-plough.com.

Scotiabank

Naomi Shaw
Global Vice President, Organization Effectiveness and
Leadership Development

Scotiabank – which celebrated its 175th anniversary in 2007 – is one of North America's premier financial institutions and Canada's most international bank. With close to 57,000 employees, Scotiabank Group and its affiliates serve approximately 12 million customers in some 50 countries around the world, offering a diverse range of products and services, including personal, commercial, corporate, and investment banking.

State Street Corporation

Wendy A. Watson
Executive Vice President, Global Services

State Street Corporation is the world's leading provider of financial services to institutional investors, including investment servicing, investment management, and investment research and trading. With US$15.1 trillion in assets under custody and US$2.0 trillion in assets under management, as of September 30, 2007, State Street operates in 26 countries and more than 100 geographic markets worldwide. For more information, visit State Street's Web site at www.statestreet.com.

The Stride Rite Corporation

Denise Lockaby
Director of Professional Development

The Stride Rite Corporation is the leading marketer of high quality children's footwear in the U.S. and is a major marketer of athletic and casual footwear for children and adults. Its business was founded on the strength of the Stride Rite® children's brand, but today includes a portfolio of great American brands addressing different market segments within the footwear industry. In addition to the Stride Rite® brand, the company markets footwear under the following owned or licensed brands: Keds®, Grasshoppers®, Robeez®, Saucony®, Hind®, Sperry Top-Sider®, and Tommy Hilfiger®.

The company is predominantly a wholesaler of footwear, selling its products nationally in a wide variety of retail formats including premier department stores, independent shoe stores, value retailers, and specialty stores. It markets products in countries outside the U.S. and Canada through independent distributors and licensees. The company imports substantially all of its products from independent resources in the Far East which manufacture footwear according to each brand's specifications and quality standards.

UBS Financial Services, Inc.

Barbara Cona Amone
Head of HR, Americas and Head of Global Talent,
UBS Investment Bank Managing Director and member of
UBS Investment Bank Board

Michelle Blieberg
Managing Director, Global Learning Officer

Barbara Fuchs
Director of Talent Development, UBS Wealth Management

UBS is one of the world's leading financial firms, serving a discerning international client base. Its business, global in scale, is focused on growth. As an integrated firm, UBS creates added value for clients by drawing on the combined resources and expertise of all its businesses.

UBS is the leading global wealth manager, a top tier investment banking and securities firm, and one of the largest global asset managers. In Switzerland, UBS is the market leader in retail and commercial banking.

UBS is present in all major financial centers worldwide. It has offices in 50 countries, with about 39 percent of its employees working in the Americas, 33 percent in Switzerland, 16 percent in the rest of Europe, and 12 percent in Asia Pacific. UBS's financial businesses employ more than 80,000 people around the world.

Assessment Tools and Approaches

This appendix provides a description of the most widely used assessment tools that are used to identity MVPs and high potential employees.

It begins with a chart that gives a brief overview of each assessment tool. The chart describes why the tool was developed, the target population of the tool, whether or not certification is required, and the contact information to enable readers to obtain more details of this tool.

Following the chart, a more detailed description of each assessment tool is given for those readers who want more information.

Tool	Why Developed	Directed Population	Administration Certification	Contact information
360° Feedback – Apex Model	Developed specifically to help senior-level executives successfully meet the challenge of providing leadership at the highest levels of management.	Senior-level executives	Required	Center for Creative Leadership Ph: 336.545.2810 E-mail: info@leaders.ccl.org Web site: www.ccl.org/lge
360° Feedback – Benchmarks	Developed as an assessment tool for individual development and as a profiling instrument for work groups.	Management and work teams	Required	Center for Creative Leadership Ph: 336.545.2810 E-mail: info@leaders.ccl.org Web site: www.ccl.org/lge
360° Feedback – VOICES	Developed to provide a powerful online tool for behavior assessment and improvement.	Individuals, teams, and management	Required	Lominger International: A Korn/Ferry Company 5051 Highway 7, Suite 100 Minneapolis, MN 55416-2291 Ph: 952.345.3600 E-mail: business_office@lominger.com Web site: www.lominger.com
Leadership Effectiveness Analysis 360 – LEA 360®	Developed to provide a behavioral description of approach to leadership to use across leadership levels, functions, industries and countries.	Mid to senior-level leaders	Required	Management Research Group 14 York Street, #301 Portland, ME 04101 Ph: 207.775.3132 Fax: 207.775.6796 E-mail: info@mrg.com Web site: www.mrg.com
Verify Ability Screening Online (ASO)	Developed for accurate online assessment of candidates.	Candidates	Required	SHL Client Support Group Ph: 1.800.899.7451 E-mail: Client.Support@shlgroup.com Web site: www.shl.com

suggesting that they need to change anything. Enhanced feedback, because of its scope and power, provides a method and process for confronting and dealing with such resistance.

The APEX Model of Enhanced 360-Degree Feedback

The *Awareness Program for Executive Excellence* or *APEX* is an enhanced feedback experience created specifically to help senior-level executives successfully meet the challenge of providing leadership at the highest levels of management. In addition to the use of standard 360-degree assessment instruments, APEX offers enhanced feedback from the following sources: detailed verbatim feedback from 20 or more personal interviews; observations from friends and family members; psychometric measures of personality, motivation, and needs; a personal and family biographical inventory; reports of team performance and satisfaction; as well as other instrumentation.

APEX is not intended to be "therapy" nor was it designed as a process to "fix" an executive with serious performance problems, although it does shed light on an executive's situation from multiple sources and perspectives. There is also an element of "readiness" or openness to learning that is crucial to this particular form of executive development. To a certain degree, the process can stimulate readiness, but the onus is clearly on the individual participant to be open to feedback and learning.

The program might best be characterized as an intense and comprehensive development vehicle that is designed to help the already successful executive maximize his or her effectiveness and impact in all of life's arenas. Success in this endeavor requires a committed involvement of the executive and his or her co-workers, working closely with a team of CCL staff to discover and then paint a portrait of the history, status, and possibilities for the individual. To achieve those possibilities, the executive – with challenge, support, and guidance from the CCL team – creates a development plan and implementation strategy. The implementation process includes ongoing coaching and progress assessment.

The ideal APEX client is an executive-level individual who is at a career/life stage in which an intensive review would be beneficial. Typically, such individuals are in the most senior level positions, and are being groomed or considered for further promotions. CCL does reserve the right to screen the candidate during the pre-assessment phase and may decline to go further in the APEX process if the pre-assessment suggests that such an intervention would be inappropriate or unlikely to be beneficial.

A note on confidentiality: Data collected is the sole property of the executive and is not shared with the home organization, except as the executive chooses to disclose. Since CCL is a research organization, permission for analysis and publication may be requested from the individual. However, neither the individual nor the sponsoring organization will be identified.

360 – Degree Assessment BENCHMARKS®

Benchmarks is a 360-degree assessment tool that offers experienced managers an in-depth look at development by assessing skills honed from a multitude of on-the-job leadership experiences. Benchmarks also helps executives identify what lessons may still need to be learned, establishes what specific work experiences need to be sought out in order to develop critical skills for success, and identifies possible problems that may stall their career.

Benchmarks is a statistically reliable, valid, and comprehensive 360-degree feedback instrument that, in addition to providing feedback to help identify strengths and developmental needs, also does what its name suggests – it provides the practicing manager with a benchmark of how he or she is doing when compared to a similar norm group. Based on the Center for Creative Leadership's studies of how successful executives develop, and why they derail, Benchmarks focuses on what can be learned from experience by:

- Providing information on potential career blocks – certain flaws or behaviors that may lead to derailment (in Benchmarks, "derailment" refers to executives who were expected to go higher in their organization but had their careers stopped involuntarily by being demoted, plateaued, or fired)
- Linking lessons and experiences together to guide further development

How Is Benchmarks Used?

Benchmarks has two general uses and functions:

1. As a confidential tool for individual development. In addition to rating themselves, managers receive feedback from superiors, peers, direct reports, and other observers. They also see themselves compared with a relevant norm. Benchmarks is appropriate for a wide range of managers – from mid-level managers to CEOs.

2. As a profiling instrument for work groups. This is used to depict where a group is strong or has developmental needs, and to show what appear to be the most salient factors for success in their environment. A group, defined by the organization, can be compared with a relevant norm.

Feedback on Benchmarks can be delivered as part of a training program or through one-to-one feedback sessions with certified professionals. An integral part of the feedback is the Development Learning Guide, which accompanies the feedback report. It provides a context for developmental planning, and explains how successful executives can develop their skills and confront their flaws.

How Was Benchmarks Developed?

Benchmarks was developed from studies of how successful managers learn, grow, and change, not from what they do or what qualities they should possess to do their jobs. Benchmarks differs from other instruments by focusing on what successful executives learned from experiences that mattered the most in their careers.

"Key Events" Studies

How do future executives develop on the job? Do certain critical experiences matter? Do these experiences, as many have said, teach valuable lessons? Seeking answers to these questions has been the subject of continuing studies at the Center for Creative Leadership (CCL) since 1982. The Key Events studies led to four major conclusions that CCL refers to as "Learning from Experience."

- Executives believe that valuable learning occurs on the job, and similar lessons (skills, values, and perspectives) were reported in every corporation studied.
- The experiences that teach these lessons also show some cohesion. Challenging job assignments, significant other people, and hardships dominate what executives and managers recall as developmental.
- There is a strong link between experiences and lessons learned. What is learned is not random; it flows from the specific experience.
- Having the experience is far from a guarantee of focused learning. Only managers who had a pattern of continuous learning remained effective.

Executive Derailment Research

A second set of studies that led to the creation and evolution of Benchmarks was on executive derailment. Successful executives were asked to think about two people they knew well – an executive who succeeded and one who had recently derailed. Similar information about both groups was collected: background, strengths and weaknesses, how they were first noticed, and how they made it to at least the general management level. For the derailed group, the flaws that led to their derailment were examined. From these data, researchers derived "fatal flaws" or reasons for derailment. These reasons provide the foundation for the items that are grouped into the "potential flaws" section of Benchmarks.

What Components and Terms Are Used in Benchmarks?

The following offers a general description of the components and an introduction to some terms.

Feedback Report

The Benchmarks Feedback Report is a 39-page report that is organized from general to specific feedback. The overview pages show average scale scores. Each scale is then broken down by rater group (boss, superior, peer, direct report, other) and presented item by item. Normative comparisons are also provided.

Sections of Benchmarks Feedback Report

Benchmarks feedback includes two sections assessing (1) the skills and perspectives related to effectiveness and (2) problems that can stall careers.

Section 1: Leadership Skills and Perspectives

The leadership skills and perspectives in Section 1 are clustered into three groupings:

1. *Meeting Job Challenges* includes scales measuring the resourcefulness needed to cope with the demands of the job, the drive and attitudes necessary, and the ability to learn and make decisions quickly. These demands include solving problems, thinking strategically, working with upper management, building structure and systems, acting with incomplete information, taking full responsibility for actions, facing adversity, and seizing opportunities.

2. *Leading People* includes scales focusing on behaviors directed toward the specific group of individuals for whom the manager is responsible as well as other people in the organization. These include setting a developmental climate for employees, sizing up potential employees, delegating and encouraging, developing shared expectations, confronting problem people, managing change initiatives, and creating a climate for participation in decision making. Accomplishing these tasks is related to the skills and perspectives inherent in the other two clusters: interpersonal skills and resourcefulness. Yet this

cluster adds unique components needed in the manager: being team-focused and having the ability to motivate others.

3. *Respecting Self and Others* includes scales focusing on compassion and sensitivity toward others, respecting differences, treating others with integrity, and putting others at ease. It also includes the ability to build cooperative relationships and handle conflicts effectively. Scales focusing on oneself also fall into this cluster – having a realistic view of one's strengths and weaknesses, proactively managing one's career, and trying to balance one's personal and work lives.

Because skills and perspectives vary in importance in different work units, respondents to Benchmarks also rate which of the skills and perspectives in Section 1 are most "Important for Success" in their particular work environments.

Section 2: Problems That Can Stall a Career

This section focuses on possible derailment factors. Items on these scales emerged from a completely separate area of research – while some of the items may correspond with certain items in Section 1, they are not just negatively worded versions of the items. For example, Problems with Interpersonal Relationships could possibly represent the negative end of the continuum represented by the Building and Mending Relationships scale in Section 1. However, looking at the actual items in these sections reveals that Building and Mending Relationships focuses on working hard to understand others, getting cooperation from peers and clients, and negotiating well. The Problems with Interpersonal Relationships scale focuses on aspects of the manager's personality, such as arrogance or adopting a bullying style under stress, that could interfere with good interpersonal relationships. These scales are related but provide different information.

Other scales in Section 2 focus on difficulties building and leading teams, difficulties changing or adapting, failing to meet business objectives, and having too narrow of a functional orientation.

Norm Groups

The meaningfulness of feedback is enhanced when a manager is able to compare his or her scores to those of similar managers. Such a comparison group is referred to as a norm group. In order to provide comparative information as part of Benchmarks feedback, data are collected from Benchmarks users on a continuous basis. The norms are updated approximately every two years.

Development Learning Guide

The Development Learning Guide provides the framework for the participant to set developmental goals and establishes strategies to reach them.

After the administration and scoring of Benchmarks, the feedback process involves a progression of steps:

- Orientation to Benchmarks: research and development of the instrument, mechanics of the report, etc.
- Individual analysis of the Benchmarks report
- One-to-one consultation with a certified feedback specialist

Whether done individually or in a group setting, orientation to Benchmarks and individual analysis require three to four hours to complete.

Further Information can be Obtained from CCL

Questions about the Benchmarks instrument should be forwarded to the Center for Creative Leadership, 336-545-2810. Or you can visit the Center for Creative Leadership's Web site at *www.ccl.org*.

VOICES® 360° Feedback System

VOICES® is a Web-enabled 360-degree feedback system that provides access to the LEADERSHIP ARCHITECT® Library of 67 Competencies, 19 Career Stallers and Stoppers, 26 Clusters and 8 Factors,

7 International Focus Areas, 10 Universal Performance Dimensions, and 356 Behavioral Aspects. You may also use your own items.

A competency-based, research-validated 360-degree assessment provides a learner (the person receiving 360-degree feedback) a powerful tool for development and improvement. Critical feedback is a must in stimulating people toward self-improvement and job and career success. The 360-degree feedback reveals how a learner's job behaviors are perceived by those around him or her and which of these behaviors are considered important for success. In addition, a learner can see how the ratings of others compare to his or her self-ratings.

Administer the VOICES® online system yourself or engage Lominger's Global Survey Center as your administrator. In either case, VOICES® is designed to be a best practice application where anonymity and data security are a must.

Features and benefits of the VOICES® online system:

- Simplified survey event setup
- Fully customizable: use any combination of Lominger's or your own items
- Three possible rating questions for VOICES®: skill, importance, overuse
- Optional pre-coding of rater relationships
- Customizable automatic e-mail invitations to learners and raters
- Customizable follow-up e-mail reminders to raters who haven't completed a pending survey
- Visual feedback to raters as they complete the survey to help them see the distribution (spread) of their ratings to encourage full use of the scale
- Easy administration authorized system users can enter the survey system from any PC with Internet access
- Up to 19 selectable report sections – including Skill-Importance Matrix Report. Report selections and sequence can be customized for each learner.
- Group reports available at no cost if self-printed
- Better, faster, ASP application (no software to install)
- Optional demographics
- Optional learner-driven rater nomination
- Real-time online status checking
- Better, faster reporting

Measure Improvement with a Development Tracker™ Mini Survey

Recent research indicates that pre- and post-360-degree efforts aren't the best measure of competency improvement efforts. We have responded to this finding by creating a survey that helps you to specifically measure the impact of a participant's awareness of his or her developmental needs and the impact that coaching or learning events had on the participant's development initiative. Launch a Development Tracker™ mini survey six to nine months after 360-degree feedback initiatives to measure skill improvement, monitor individual development progress, or assess return on investment (ROI) to help you track the bottom-line impact of your feedback, coaching, and development initiatives.

Leadership Effectiveness Analysis (LEA)

The LEA was developed by the company Management Research Group (MRG).

Since 1983, MRG has developed products, research, solutions, and services for the development of more meaningful and effective organizational leadership. Their assessment instruments are built using a *unique design* and *leading-edge research* and are delivered in a wide offering of *languages*. Independent consultants combine their expertise with MRG's products and services to ensure the delivery of powerful solutions.

MRG is unique among assessment companies for these reasons:

- Research is its foundation.
- MRG's unique assessment design results in feedback that is non-biased, descriptive, practical, and robust.
- Their database is one of the largest in the industry.
- Assessment and feedback are linked to a company's strategic context, making the results truly meaningful and applicable to the organization's needs.

The LEA can be used in two ways – either as a self assessment or as a 360 assessment. Both types of LEA assessments provide valid and reliable feedback from self and others – direct reports, peers, and bosses – on the use of leadership behaviors. LEA 360™ produces a rich feedback report complete with profiles, narratives, strategic implications, and developmental opportunities. Because the feedback is based on behaviors, change and improvement efforts are realistic and tangible. The LEA Resource Guide, included with the feedback report, suggests action steps and provides tools for prioritizing and focusing developmental actions.

The LEA provides feedback on 22 leadership practices which are clustered into six key clusters: Creating a Vision, Developing Followership, Implementing the Vision, Following Through, Achieving Results, and Team Playing.

SHL Verify

SHL Verify includes a range of online ability tests to measure verbal, numerical, and inductive reasoning ability. As SHL Verify is a sophisticated package that includes innovative psychometrics, robust technology and industry-first data security and forensics, SHL Verify protects the integrity of online assessment and ensures the process is fair and the results are accurate.

Benefits

- Protects against the risks of cheating and security breaches
- Defends the integrity of online testing by partnering with independent security and data forensic experts
- Utilises randomised test technology that produces a unique set of items for each test, ensuring that every individual who takes the test receives a different test
- Superior test properties make SHL Verify the most powerful online tests range available today, which leads to better decisions
- Pioneers breakthrough psychometrics which scientifically verify the integrity of unsupervised online test results and leads to process efficiency gains
- Supported by leading-edge technology that underpins the science
- Cuts the time and effort involved in re-testing applicants and creates significant process efficiencies for employers.

By capturing the benefits of online testing, while overcoming the risks that other assessment systems cannot, SHL Verify provides benefits above and beyond all other testing methods – online or offline.

SHL Verify Range of Ability Test details

Tests available: Verbal (17-19mins*), Numeric (17-25mins*) and Inductive Reasoning (25mins*).

Verification tests: Verbal (11mins*), Numerical (14-15mins*), Inductive Reasoning (7mins*)
* *Verify offers tests at different job levels and the time for Verify tests varies depending on the level of the test used.*

Comparison groups for each test are available across the following industry sectors:
- Banking, finance, and professional services
- Retail, hospitality, and leisure
- Engineering, science, and technology
- Public sector/government
- General population

SHL Verify is currently available in U.K. and U.S. English for the verbal and numerical reasoning tests and U.K. English for the inductive reasoning test, with many more language versions currently under development.

For the latest Verify availability information, or to find out more about other SHL products or services, please make a product enquiry with your local SHL office.

To see example questions or practice an online ability test, go to www.shldirect.com

BarOn EQ

A growing body of research suggests that emotional intelligence is a key determinant of success in life. Based on over 20 years of research by Dr Reuven BarOn and tested on over 85,000 individuals worldwide, BarOn EQ-i® is the first measure of emotional intelligence to be reviewed in the *BUROS Mental Measurement Yearbook* (the leading international review of psychometric tests).

Key Features

- Self-report and 360-degree versions available
- Paper and pencil, PC or online assessment
- Relatively short questionnaire for such in-depth coverage of the area (125 or 133 items)
- Large body of evidence confirming its reliability and validity

What the Baron EQ-i Measures

The BarOn EQ-i consists of 133 items and takes approximately 30 minutes to complete. It gives an overall EQ score as well as scores for the following five composite scales and 15 subscales:

Intrapersonal:

Self-Regard
Emotional Self-Awareness
Assertiveness
Independence
Self-Actualization

Interpersonal:

Empathy
Social Responsibility
Interpersonal Relationship

Adaptability:

Reality Testing
Flexibility
Problem Solving

Stress Management:

Stress Tolerance
Impulse Control

General Mood:

Optimism
Happiness

Benefits for the Organization

- Identifies development needs and under-utilized strengths for individuals, creating more competent and motivated staff
- Enhances the quality of communication throughout the organization
- Acts as a catalyst for changing organizational culture
- Clearer assessment of development needs in "people skills" for the organization
- Useful for more effective team functioning

Benefits for the Individual

- Identifies individual development needs
- Highlights individual's strengths
- Suggests a range of development strategies
- Creates a basis for discussion between individuals and their colleagues, assisting personal development

California Personality Inventory™ Tool (CPI™)

The California Psychological Inventory™ (CPI™) instrument provides a complex yet highly accurate portrait of an individual's professional and personal styles. For more than 50 years, coaches, counselors, and human resource experts have trusted this powerful assessment tool to help them create efficient and productive organizations, promote teamwork, build leadership competencies, and find and develop employees who are destined for success. With 434 items, the CPI instrument provides unmatched validity and reliability as a dynamic and objective measure of personality and behavior. The complete collection of tools includes narrative reports; comparative profiles based on both gender-specific and combined male/female norms; and a comprehensive tool kit of in-depth case studies and reproducible masters that demonstrate how the CPI assessment can be used in any business or organizational setting.

CPI™ 434 Narrative Report (C)

This comprehensive report provides you with a well-organized narrative interpretation of your client's CPI™ 434 results. It includes a *Profile* of your client's CPI™ type, level, and Folk Scales results, and then elaborates on that information in narrative form for a comprehensive CPI™ interpretation. The *Narrative Report* includes all 100 California Q-sort items, from the most descriptive to the least descriptive, which make predictive statements about your client's behavior to aid your interpretation, helping you describe your client in a close, knowledgeable, and objective manner.

This report includes two scale profiles, one for the gender-specific norm group and one with total norms (combined male/female norms) for use in employment situations when gender-neutral norms are needed. The *Narrative Report* measures your client's potential leadership abilities and creative potential, which makes it highly useful in business settings. It also measures your client's results on several Special Purpose Scales, including creative temperament, managerial potential, and tough-mindedness.

CPI™ 434 Profile (C)

The CPI™ *Profile* is a clear and organized presentation of your client's CPI™ type, level, and Folk Scales scores. It provides a snapshot of CPI™ 434 results, highlighting the important elements, which allows for quick and easy interpretation. The organization of the *Profile* saves you time by providing all the information you need to prepare your own narrative interpretation for the client. In addition to a gender-specific profile, the CPI™ *Profile* includes a total profile (combined male/female norms) for use in employment situations when gender-neutral reporting is required. It also provides your client's scores on seven Special Purpose Scales, including creative temperament, managerial potential, work orientation, leadership potential, amicability, tough-mindedness, and law enforcement orientation.

CPI™ Configural Analysis Report (C)

Beginning with the five parts of the CPI™ *Narrative Report*-type and level information, Folk Scales plots for gender and total/combined norms, individual Folk Scales in a narrative format, and a personalized ranking of the 100 Q-sort items. The *Configural Analysis Report* builds on that information by providing two types of interpretations based on combinations of scales: (1) empirical analyses derived from research; and (2) speculative analyses derived from interpretations by the author or his colleagues.

Based on the author's book, *A Practical Guide to CPI™ Interpretation*, the *Configural Analysis Report* saves considerable time by scanning the client's Folk Scales results, looking for only those reasonable and useful components that could be found by McAllister's list of more than 150 interpretations. The search is done for you, and the comments are listed in order and separated into "Empirical" and "Speculative" sections.

Critical Thinking Test (CTT)

The Critical Thinking Test (CTT) is the first of a new breed of shortened ability tests that provide clients with the capability to assess candidates in verbal and numerical reasoning more quickly than many existing ability tests on the market, while at the same time retaining all the rigor and reliability that clients expect from SHL.

The CTT is the latest test within the Management and Graduate Item Bank designed for the assessment of graduates, managers, and professional staff in a wide range of positions. The CTT has the most extensive set of norm data available having been drawn from over 23,000 people's data across 95 occupational groups.

Suitable for: Middle Managers, Senior Managers, Management Trainees, Graduates

NCT1 Numerical Critical Reasoning

Measures the ability to make correct decisions or inferences from numerical data. The task set and data presented are highly relevant to a range of management level jobs. Candidates may use calculator, which further increases job relevance and puts emphasis clearly on understanding and evaluation rather than computation.

Time: 35 minutes

VCT1 Verbal Critical Reasoning

Measures the ability to evaluate the logic of various kinds of arguments. The task set and topics covered are designed to be relevant to managerial work, enhancing the suitability of the test for use with professionals and managers.

Time: 25 minutes

DISC

D: Dominance; I: Influence; S: Steady; C: Compliance (DISC)

Dominance. Focus is on problems and how the individual deals with challenges. How the individual approaches and responds to problems and challenges and exercises power.

Influence. Focus is on people and how the individual deals with contacts/interaction. How the individual interacts with and attempts to influence others to their point of view.

Steady. Focus is on pace and how the individual deals with consistency. How individual responds to change, variation, and pace of their environment.

Compliance. Focus is on procedures and how the individual deals with constraints. How individual responds to rules and procedures set by others and to authority.

- DISC is a behaviorally-based assessment that is also used as a communication tool.

- DISC measures your natural style and your adapted style. Your natural style is who you are when you are relaxed (outside of work), your adapted style reflects how your style changes – or "adapts" – to the work environment.

Objectives of DISC are:

- Understand your own communication style
- Learn how to understand and read the communication style of others
- Adapt your style in order to communicate more effectively with others
- The language of DISC is universal, observable, and most importantly neutral in meaning (there is no right or wrong style)
- While each individual has a core style, most people are a blend of all four
- DISC has an 85 percent predictive accuracy

DISC does NOT measure:

- Intelligence
- Values
- Skills and Experience
- Education and Training
- Personality

When it was created and why:

- The major developer of the DISC language (Dominance, Influencing, Steadiness, and Compliance) is Dr. William Mouton Marston (1893-1947).
- Walter Clark was the first to develop an instrument.
- Bill J. Bonnstetter validated communication style.
- The DISC language is based on observable behavior.
- The DISC measurement system reveals strengths and weaknesses, one's actual behavior and tendencies towards certain

behavior. Research suggests that the most effective people are those who understand themselves and others. The more one understands personal strengths and weaknesses coupled with the ability to identify and understand the strengths and weaknesses of others, the better one will be able to develop strategies to meet the demands of the environment.

Audience for the tool:

- Anyone who would like to improve their communication style
- Managers, leaders, sales professionals

When it is useful:

- Gaining commitment and cooperation
- Building effective teams
- Resolving and preventing conflict
- Gaining endorsement (or gaining credibility or influence)
- Increasing sales

Employee Potential Assessment Tool Report Corporate Leadership Council®

Employee potential is the combination of three distinct and often disparate qualities of employees – ability, engagement, and aspiration – that increase an employee's likelihood of succeeding in a more senior position. The effective management of employee potential is a critical component to building an organization's future leadership capabilities; the Council designed this tool to give members the critical measures of employee potential and the organization's ability to develop top talent.

The Employee Potential Assessment Tool (EPAT) is an online survey that measures employee potential, targets employee development strategies, and assesses the organization's effectiveness in providing the best developmental experiences.

Based upon the Council's research, *Realizing the Full Potential of Rising Talent*, the tool answers three common questions regarding the management of employee potential:

- How much potential do my employees have?
- Which development experiences will help my employees best realize their potential?
- How effective are we at developing potential in our employees?

Participation in EPAT consists of six steps:

1. **Signing Up for a Scheduled Assessment Window:** Council members who wish to use the tool may sign up for a scheduled assessment window – a period of time for employees and their managers to take an online survey.

2. **Selecting the Employees to Participate:** Working with Council staff, members select which employees and their managers will participate. Some companies will choose to survey their already-identified HIPO employees, while many others will choose to survey a broader subsection of their employee base. Once chosen, members give the Council select information about the employees and their managers, including their e-mail addresses.

3. **Communicating with Employees and Their Managers:** Members communicate to their respondents in advance of the survey window to inform them of the upcoming survey, answer their questions, and urge their participation. (Communication templates are available form the Council.)

4. **Launching the Survey Window:** On the opening day of the survey window, members send a password protected link to the Web site to the designated employees and their managers. Survey windows will vary in length according to member preferences and sample size.

5. **Sending Reminders:** During the survey window, members may choose to send reminders to their respondents to increase response rates using templates and examples provided by the Council.

6. **Access the Report and Analysis:** Members will be sent a customized report and analysis of their data within 20 business days of the close of the survey window.

Both the individual and their manager fill out the online potential tool. Managers assess their direct reports ability. The employees assess themselves and their experiences. The resulting reports provide the organization with the following:

- Data and benchmarks of individual employee potential levels
- Recommendations on best to develop employee potential

The employee potential tool is included in CLC membership at no additional cost.

To access the research and find out details of the tool go to www.clc.executiveboard.com.

Membership of the CLC is required in order to access the site.

The Leadership Report

Based on responses to both the FIRO-B® and MBTI® instruments, this report helps clients explore and expand their understanding of the leadership style they use in organizations and how others might perceive and react to it. Both instruments tap into key aspects of personality and behavior in areas such as communication, problem solving, decision making, and interpersonal relations. Together, they complement each other and provide rich information of use in a personal, ongoing leadership development program. The Coach's Guide to the Leadership Report provides all the background information needed to present the report to the client: summary points about FIRO-B and MBTI type theory; tips on interpreting and presenting the results; and a complete explanation of the logic underlying the report, potential issues in interpretation, and what to emphasize.

Hogan Personality Inventory (HPI)

The HPI is used as a measure of how the leader will routinely operate under normal circumstances. The HPI provides information regarding the "bright side" of personality. These are characteristics that appear during social interaction and that facilitate or inhibit a person's ability to: (a) get along with others and (b) achieve his or her goals. The HPI is useful in counseling an individual when he or she may be unaware of a feature of his or her style of interacting with others that does or can create difficulty in the work place. This instrument is completed within 20-30 minutes online by the leader. A paper copy of the report is provided for review with the leader. An electronic copy of the report will also be provided.

Hogan Development Survey (HDS)

The HDS reveals the extent to which the leader has one or more of the eleven common performance risks that can interfere with his or her ability to build relationships with others and create cohesive, goal-oriented teams. We will apply the information on potential "derailers" in preparing development suggestions.

While the characteristics revealed in HPI are easily seen in day-to-day behavior, the performance risks assessed by the HDS will only be seen in situations where the leader is not actively managing his or her public image. These situations might include those involving high stress or change, multi-tasking, poor person-job fit, or when a person's comfort with those with whom he or she works leads the person to no longer manage his or her public image. This instrument is completed within 20-30 minutes on-line by the leader. A paper copy of the report is provided for review with the leader. An electronic copy of the report will also be provided.

You will benefit from it, no matter who you are – or where you are in your career.

You may be a new manager – and you may want to get a jump-start to help you be a better leader right from the beginning.

You may be midway through your career, or even later. And right about now, you may want a reality check to make absolutely certain that you are living up to your potential, which was, after all, the reason you were hired.

You could even be a senior executive looking for some straight, unbiased feedback about how you lead.

The Looking Glass Experience

The Looking Glass Experience can show you how you lead and influence others in an organization. You will learn how to make difficult, complex decisions – and you will learn how your particular leadership style affects your workplace, those you work with and, ultimately, your own success as a leader.

The Looking Glass, Inc.® organizational simulation is successful because it is real. It so closely parallels real life that you will find that your performance mirrors the behaviors you exhibit at work. It can lead to a dramatic improvement in your strategic thinking process, along with your ability to communicate, successfully navigate the complexities of your organization and foster productive relationships.

At the end of it, you can expect to see the real you. And that's good. The best way to improve what you see when you look at yourself in the future is to get an accurate picture of what you look like right now.

Who Should Attend

Mid- to senior-level managers who oversee people, projects or both, who want to improve their leadership abilities by participating in a feedback-intense, action-learning organizational simulation.

Outcomes

- Develop the ability to recognize opportunities and avoid pitfalls, balance tactical concerns with strategic possibilities and become better at making decisions.
- Gain a more complete view of yourself, including strengths and developmental needs, within the context of your organization.
- Set specific goals that will help you more successfully navigate complex leadership situations.
- Gain self-awareness on how to best adapt to complex organizational challenges and the effect they have on productivity.
- Learn to take on new roles, communicate more effectively at all levels and receive constructive feedback.
- Receive direct, applicable insight of the complexities involved in managing a global enterprise.

Myers – Briggs Type Inventory

MBTI® Step II Interpretive Report – Form Q

The *Step II Interpretive Report* is a highly personalized narrative and graphic report that helps clients understand and apply their MBTI® results. It can be generated on the basis of either the client's reported type (results from scoring the items) or his or her verified type (if your client has previously taken the MBTI® instrument and verified his or her best-fit type). If you use verified type, Form Q item responses are also required.

The *Step II Interpretive Report* offers Step I results and describes in detail the client's four-letter personality type. Next, his or her Step II facet results are displayed graphically. Personalized text explains the client's result on each of the 20 facets. These results are then applied to four important components of executive development: communication, change management, decision making, and conflict management. The report describes your client's style in these four areas and suggests ways of using that style more effectively.

This report integrates Step I and Step II results to help clients see how their facet results affect their personality type. The interpreter's summary shows the client's results in brief; the average range of scores of people of the client's MBTI® type; and the polarity index, a measure of the consistency of Form Q responses.

Organizational Savvy Self-Assessment

Under-political people equate all company politics with evil, sleazy tactics and avoid entering the arena at all. They often wind up surrendering power, influence, and resources to overly political colleagues. Now you can assess your current ability to use *ethical political savvy* and learn how to gain organizational impact with integrity.

What is the Organizational Savvy Self-Assessment? A quick screening tool to survey your abilities in 12 categories of *high-integrity organizational politics*.

Who Is It Aimed At? The *Self-Assessment* is meant for executives, managers, professionals, or individual contributors who want to measure their skill level and better understand the components of ethical politics on the job and in other organizational settings.

Do I Need the Book to Benefit? No. People often complete the instrument after reading *Survival of the Savvy* in order to reinforce what they have learned, set goals, and monitor their progress. Others use the *Self-Assessment* to identify their strengths and weaknesses, glean quick tips for improvement, and get a clear sense of how the book will help them hone their skills in specific areas. Each savvy skill set on the *Self-Assessment* corresponds to one or more chapters in the book, but the two resources have stand-alone benefit.

What's the Take-Away Value? First, you'll discover any blind spots you have in the arena of organizational politics. You will also learn many components of organizational savvy simply by rating yourself on each skill set item. Finally, regardless of how well you currently function, the recommendations for improvement in the *Interpretation Guide* will kick-start your journey to more successful navigation of organizational politics.

The *Organizational Savvy Self-Assessment* is a 60-item rating instrument that yields an overall organizational savvy score and 12 separate skill set scores. The 15-page *Scoring and Interpretation Guide* provides a profile of your strong points and gaps. For each of the 12 savvy skill sets, you'll receive analysis that includes:

- Your skill set score and rating as proficient, capable, or vulnerable
- A review of the five assessment items that comprise the skill set
- An explanation of the skill set's purpose and impact
- Specific pointers and recommendations for improvement
- A list of related chapters in the book, *Survival of the Savvy*

SOCIAL STYLE Model™

The SOCIAL STYLE Model™ is a tool for understanding our basic behaviors and the impact we have on others. It's the most rigorously tested and practical approach for identifying and building interpersonal skills in business settings, with a nearly 50-year record of proven success.

What's Your SOCIAL STYLE(sm)?

Understanding behaviors doesn't have to be complicated. TRACOM's research-based SOCIAL STYLE Model™ breaks down typical behaviors into four social styles: driving, expressive, amiable and analytical.

Everyone has natural behavioral patterns. Generally speaking, we fall into one of four categories, or social styles. SOCIAL STYLE is determined by gaging a person on two dimensions of human behavior: assertiveness and responsiveness.

- **Assertiveness** is the degree to which you tend to ask or tell during interactions. (e.g., Do you quietly ask your colleagues "Would you like to go to lunch?" or loudly announce "Let's go to lunch!"?)
- **Responsiveness** is the degree to which you tend to control or emote. (e.g., If you're angry, do you keep it to yourself or let everyone know how you feel?)

The combination of your assertive and responsive tendencies reveals your SOCIAL STYLE(sm):

- **Analytical** (Ask Assertive + Control Responsive): serious, exacting, logical; values accuracy and facts
- **Driving** (Tell Assertive + Control Responsive): independent, practical, formal; values actions and results
- **Expressive** (Tell Assertive + Emote Responsive): animated, forceful, impulsive; values approval and spontaneity
- **Amiable** (Ask Assertive + Emote Responsive): dependable, open, supportive; values security and relationships

A few things to remember:

- None of the social styles are inherently good or bad; all have strengths and weaknesses.
- Your SOCIAL STYLE is not as important as how you use it. (Read about Versatility)
- Social styles are themes of behavior. We all have characteristics of each style, and the categories are not absolute. However, individuals generally have one dominant style, and others come to expect certain types of behaviors from them.
- Because of the significant differences in the four styles, natural conflict occurs in daily interactions. Building familiarity and comfort with the behaviors of each style allows people to work

better with colleagues of all styles. Current organizational development/organizational effectiveness research continues to support TRACOM's research that social and self-awareness is key to interpersonal success. (e.g., Daniel Goleman's *Emotional Intelligence* and Steven Covey's *7 Habits of Highly Successful People*.)

Unlike most training, the SOCIAL STYLE Model™ can be applied daily in an endless number of situations. It's useful any time you need to work with others to accomplish a result. SOCIAL STYLE concepts are often integrated into training programs covering topics from leadership to customer service to team development.

Components of Versatility – Research shows that people consider four basic elements when determining an individual's versatility:

- **Image:** Dress, grooming, and appearance can be critical to making good first impressions. It's not necessarily how well you're dressed, but whether you're appropriate for the situation. You may lose as much credibility wearing a tux to the company picnic as wearing sweatpants to the board meeting.

- **Presentation:** Our ability to verbally communicate with others is very important. People are more likely to trust us if we present clear, well-organized ideas and use vocabulary appropriate to the circumstances.

- **Breadth of Competence and Understanding:** It's obvious that showing competence and understanding in your work will help you gain respect. But it's also important to notice what others are interested in, and be able to discuss those topics. The ability to listen and learn helps to build common ground, leading to mutual productivity.

- **Feedback:** In this two-way process, people send and receive both verbal and non-verbal signals to gain mutual understanding. Make sure you are clear in your communication and sensitive to the signals of others in order to minimize confusion.

Versatility Ratings

By completing a TRACOM self-assessment or multi-rater assessment instrument, individuals receive low, medium or high versatility ratings. This score creates a generalization about how you will handle the tension of interpersonal relationships. Are your actions typically focused on your own comfort level, or are you concerned about the tension your behavior can create in others, causing you to vary your actions to create productive relationships?

A person of any style can have low or high versatility. Versatility obviously includes an element of personal judgment on the part of the observers. In assessing your rating, remember to consider the rating source, the person rated, and the situation surrounding the person's activities.

Thomas-Kilmann Conflict Mode Instrument (A)

The TKI allows trainers and HR professionals to safely open a discussion about conflict, to reveal patterns, and look at instances when one conflict behavior is productive and when choosing another style would be more effective.

Using the TKI has never been easier than with this new online method. Your clients will find taking the TKI online to be a fast and engaging activity. And, unlike many tools available on the Internet, the TKI is psychometrically sound and thoroughly researched, so you can trust the results your clients will receive. If you so choose, clients can receive immediate feedback, and/or results can be sent directly to you. You can conduct training using your own TKI materials or purchase materials through SkillsOne.com.

The *Thomas-Kilmann Conflict Mode Instrument Profile and Interpretive Report* follows the same basic format as the best-selling paper-and-pencil version but is tailored specifically to each individual participant. Each personalized report shows graphically how the participant uses the five conflict-handling modes:

- *Competing*: High assertiveness and low cooperativeness. The goal is "to win."
- *Avoiding*: Low assertiveness and low cooperativeness. The goal is "to delay."
- *Compromising*: Moderate assertiveness and moderate cooperativeness. The goal is "to find a middle ground."
- *Collaborating*: High assertiveness and high cooperativeness. The goal is "to find a win-win solution."

- *Accommodating*: Low assertiveness and high cooperativeness. The goal is "to yield."

Based on the participant's particular use of each approach (high, average, or low), the report offers specific suggestions to help him or her understand the pluses and minuses of a particular conflict-handling style, with suggestions for considering alternative approaches.

Help your Clients See Through Conflict to Resolution

The TKI is the number-one best-selling instrument for conflict resolution. This easy-to-use, self-scoring exercise is fast and powerful. Participants select responses from 30 statement pairs to discover which of five conflict-handling styles is their preferred "mode." Interpretation and feedback materials help clients learn about the most appropriate uses for each mode and how to increase their comfort level with·their less-used modes.

Used as a stand-alone tool by individuals, in a group learning process, or as a part of a structured workshop, the TKI is a practical approach to conflict resolution. Its simple-to-use format and easy-to-understand content have made it the centerpiece of training programs over a wide variety of applications. The companion video *Dealing with Conflict* and the *Conflict Workshop Facilitator's Guide* provide additional information and support.

Product Highlights

- Enables a facilitator to safely open productive dialogue about conflict
- Provides an easy-to-use, self-scoring exercise that takes just 15 minutes
- Explains conflict behaviors in five easy-to-understand modes
- Instructs clients about the most appropriate uses for each conflict-handling mode
- Is the most widely used conflict management assessment available

Index